P9-EMK-440

William Penn

Other Books
by Catherine O. Peare

Rosa Bonheur

Jules Verne

Stephen Foster

Henry Wadsworth Longfellow

Robert Louis Stevenson

Louisa May Alcott

Mark Twain

Washington Irving

Charles Dickens

•

Albert Einstein

William Penn

William Penn

Catherine Owens Peare

Illustrated by Henry C. Pitz

Holt, Rinehart and Winston
New York · Chicago · San Francisco

IN CANADA, HOLT, RINEHART AND
WINSTON, OF CANADA, LIMITED

LIBRARY OF CONGRESS CATALOG CARD NUMBER: 58-6513

PUBLISHED, APRIL, 1958
SECOND PRINTING, OCTOBER, 1961
THIRD PRINTING, JUNE, 1965
FOURTH PRINTING, JUNE, 1966
FIFTH PRINTING, DECEMBER, 1966
SIXTH PRINTING, AUGUST, 1967

9545401

PRINTED IN THE UNITED STATES OF AMERICA

Acknowledgments

The author wishes to thank the following for permission to use their resources in writing this book:

The Historical Society of Pennsylvania, Philadelphia, Pennsylvania, for extensive use of its large manuscript collection.

The Library, Friends House, London, for the use of its manuscripts and for permission to quote from *The Journal of George Fox,* edited by John L. Nickalls, 1952.

Friends Historical Association, Swarthmore, Pennsylvania, for permission to quote from *My Irish Journal* by William Penn, 1952.

Barnes & Noble, Inc. for permission to quote from *Narratives of Early Maryland,* 1910.

Contents

William Penn

CHAPTER ONE

Civil Wars

MRS. PENN'S EYES WERE RED-RIMMED from loss of sleep, but she would not leave the baby's side.

The maidservant stole close and touched her arm. "Please, Madam," she pleaded. "If you would rest, I can watch the boy."

Mrs. Penn brushed her aside. She went on staring at the three-year-old boy who burned with fever and sometimes waked to whimper from the pain and itch of the smallpox.

"If he survives this night," said the young mother, "we can hope."

"Please, Madam, may I go out?"

Mrs. Penn looked up and smiled in spite of her fatigue. The girl was only thirteen, bound out to service by her parents for a few shillings a year. She was wearing a discarded dress that her mistress had given her, and it made her look older.

"Go to bed," said Mrs. Penn. "The streets are filled with danger."

With a look of disappointment, the maid obeyed.

Margaret Penn sighed and pushed back the curls her maid had tried to arrange for her a little while ago. Everyone's servants were out in the streets these days—and nights—for the excitement, the riots, the rowdy crowds, a chance to throw stones or get into a fight. There would be no sleep or rest in London while the military commotions lasted.

A sudden uproar of men's voices in front of the house sent Margaret Penn hurrying to the window. She turned pale with fright as she looked down on the heads of some laborers who had just come from a tavern, pushing and jostling, tipsy to the last man. Heart pounding, she ran down the stairs to the street floor and slid the heavy bolt into place in the door and checked all the windows—then back up the stairs to her son.

If only her husband were here! If only the baby's father would come home from sea! Heaven only knew where the English fleet was now. If only the night would be over!

The boy stirred and began to cry hoarsely. She knew that his throat was sore. She sat down beside him to lay a fresh cold cloth on his forehead.

"Sh-h-h, my son. Hush, little Bille."

The child dozed off again in spite of the noise outside. Margaret Penn heard the crowd grow larger and heard the clanking swords and stamp of heavy boots on the cobblestones. She knew that soldiers were fighting with the laborers. They were probably some ex-soldiers who had been dismissed from the army without their pay. Many of them roamed the streets angrily robbing and plundering and fighting.

How much more could England stand? There had been four years of civil war between King Charles I and his Royalist followers and Cromwell with his Puritan followers. Cromwell and the Parliament had grown so strong that the King had fled to Scotland, leaving his opponents in control.

The baby slept; the mother's head nodded and soon she, too, was asleep. When she awoke with a start, the candle had burned down and gone out, and the first faint streak of daylight showed through the chinks in the shutter.

She went to the window, pushed open the shutter, and looked down into the narrow street. The city was still filled with commotion. A group of young boys dressed in knee breeches, tunics buttoned up the front, and shoes with large buckles, were walking by. They were apprentices on their way to work, and she could tell from their faces that they had been on the prowl for mischief all night. A sooty chimney sweep walked by, carrying his blackened broom.

She looked up and down in vain for a peddler walking beside a two-wheeled donkey cart. Peddlers brought much of the day's food—especially milk—from the country, but there would be none today because the city gates were barricaded. Margaret Penn felt suddenly tired of city life. She longed for the soft green hills of Ireland where she had lived as a girl.

She returned to watch her son, and as the morning light began to fill the room she noticed tiny beads of perspiration on his lip. The fever had broken! There was a chance! If the fever had continued, he would have sunk into a coma, and that would have been the end. Now there was a chance that he would live!

Kneeling down beside his bed, she prayed desperately, watching all the while. When he stirred and opened his eyes, she began to cry happily.

The days passed swiftly after that. Somehow the maidservant always managed to find something for them to eat. Once she came triumphantly home with a joint of mutton. Another time she brought a fresh carp from the fishmonger on the quay.

A large army under General Fairfax marched right into the city without any battle at all, and soon order began to be restored. The gates of the city were opened wide each morning, and life returned to something like normal. The city was still noisy, but the commotions were happier. Men on horseback galloped and clattered along. Ladies whisked by in carriages. The hucksters shouted up at the windows that they had something to sell, and they had everything imaginable . . . a man with a sack of small coals on his back, a water carrier, a knife grinder, a donkey cart full of apples, a young girl with buckets of fresh milk—all milled along with the busy crowd.

Small William Penn recovered slowly from the smallpox. He was still weak and pale, but smiling and happy, when the exciting day happened that he and his mother both waited for. His father returned from sea!

A thundering knock on the door, and he came striding into the house, filling everyone with excitement. He took his wife in his arms and whirled her around. Then he bounded up the stairs three at a time to see his first-born son. William Penn, Senior, was so used to shouting orders to seamen in a high wind that his voice boomed when he was indoors.

He picked up William Penn, Junior, and held him in his arms.

"What's this?" he demanded as he stroked the boy's head. The boy had no hair at all. The fever had burned it off.

"We can have him fitted for a wig," said the father. "Nothing so fancy as mine, though."

As he rocked his son back and forth he talked to his wife.

"I was under arrest for a few days!"

She gasped and held her hands to her mouth.

"Oh, the matter is finished. I am to be restored to my command as Rear Admiral. Cromwell must know I am a royalist, loyal to my king. But he cannot dismiss his naval officers so easily. I shall go on serving England."

He looked down at the boy in his arms and tried to speak softly, although it could scarcely have been called soft.

"My little son," said Rear Admiral Penn, "your grandfather Giles Penn was a devoted and loyal friend of Charles I, and so am I, and so are you."

Then he looked happily at his wife. There was to be no more city life for her, he told her, and no more city sicknesses for Bille. They were moving to a house in the country. Mrs. Penn hugged her husband happily, and the boy clapped his hands and laughed.

Soon after that they did move out of London, in a tall carriage drawn by horses. Their belongings were piled into open wagons and followed behind.

Mrs. Penn took one last look at the home they were leaving. It was a tall, narrow house. The street floor had a hall and parlor and kitchen, the next floor two large chambers, the next two more chambers, and above all that there was a garret. The house stood on Tower Hill, just inside the London Wall.

Her son had been born there, October 14, 1644, when her husband was still a captain. Luckily, Captain Penn had been able to pay a visit home in time to see his brand-new son. He had remained home long enough to carry the new baby to the nearby church of

All Hallows Barking-by-the-Tower and have him baptized in the Anglican faith. The Anglican Church was the official church of England, or was until Cromwell came into power.

The carriage took the Penns out through one of the northern gates of the city, along the Ongar Road for about ten miles, through the forests of Essex County, until they reached the Parish of Wanstead. There they moved into a big country house with plenty of room indoors and plenty of clean, fresh air out-of-doors. They had maidservants to look after the housecleaning, cooking, pickling and preserving, salting of fish and smoking of meat, making of wines and candles. Women usually knew about using herbs for medicine, too. Menservants took care of the horses, cows and sheep, the plowing and planting. There was forest all around them where the men could hunt for game.

Of course, the boy thrived at Wanstead. He grew sturdy and husky, and his parents realized that some day he would be tall and handsome like his father. He was full of his father's energy; his father's moods soon became his. He was warm, excitable, lovable, impatient.

Even though they were out in the quiet, peaceful countryside, news of what was going on in the world still reached the Penns. England had been suffering from civil wars for many years. There were those who supported the King and wanted him to rule like an absolute monarch as of old. There were others, chiefly the Puritans, who were beginning to think that people should be self-governing. They supported the Parliament and believed that the Parliament, elected by the people, should have a strong voice in the government. But they were way ahead of their times. That would not happen for many more years. Feelings were deep and bitter on both sides. England would have to live through more bloodshed.

When William Penn was four years old, the news reached his family that the King's armies had been defeated for the last time. The King had been taken captive. Later they heard the worst news of all. The King had been beheaded. Charles I was no more. The Puritans were in complete control, and Oliver Cromwell, the popular army general, was the most influential man in England. All those who had been loyal to the King could look forward to difficult times. The Prince of Wales, who would some day be King Charles II, fled to Holland.

"The dignity of the English Crown has been violated," declared Rear Admiral Penn. "But I can still serve England."

And so William Penn, Senior, continued to go to sea, and William Penn, Junior, began to learn his letters at home. There were no kindergartens in the seventeenth century. A child had to know his letters and numbers before he went to school. A favorite way was with a hornbook. That was a piece of board shaped like a paddle with the alphabet painted on it in black. It was covered with a thin sheet of animal horn, oiled to make it transparent.

When young William was six his father came home one day to announce that he had been promoted to vice admiral—in command of England's third fleet—with orders to proceed to the Mediterranean.

With a hearty laugh and a great wave of his arm he was gone again, galloping down Ongar Road to London, the great plume in his hat waving and bouncing in the breeze.

"Come home soon! Come home soon!" called his son after him.

The household settled down to wait for him, and Margaret Penn settled down to wait for her next baby. Thirteen months later, when Vice Admiral Penn returned once more to his wife and son and six-month-old daughter, he was a national hero.

"We sailed as far as Malta," he told them, "and we were the first English fleet to do that since the Crusades. Now the whole Mediterranean is open for English commerce."

Seven-year-old William gazed at his father with adoration. This was *his* hero, too, this man who stomped up and down the room in his wide-topped boots, britches, and doublet, and flung his big gauntlets into a corner.

And that was how life went on for the Penns. There was always a long period of peace and quiet, then home came the head of the family with great commotion and tales of adventure to tell his family and friends.

"We gave the Dutch fleet a real thrashing!" he boasted one time.

And another, "I've been made General at Sea!"

"That's the highest rank there is!" shouted his son.

Sometimes General Penn invited crowds of his seafaring friends and fellow naval officers to dinner. Sizzling roasts of meat and wild birds—ducks, quail, partridge—were set on the table on polished pewter platters. And there were big tankards of ale and fine wine, pickled rabbit, and eel pie.

William Penn could stand near his father and watch the men eating great mouthfuls and listen to the roar of deep voices. Some day he would be able to eat as heartily as his father! Some day his voice would be deep and booming!

Only four miles from Wanstead, in the village of Chigwell, there was a grammar school where William Penn began his real studies.

"It's a splendid school!" said General Penn. "That's why I have chosen it."

The school building was rectangular, made of red brick, two stories high. Like the Wanstead house, it was surrounded by the forests of Essex County. The ceilings inside were held up with heavy oak beams, and the classroom was dingy and gloomy. Small windows, high up on the walls, let in just a little daylight. The boys sat on long, backless benches, and the schoolmaster sat behind his desk up on a platform.

Classes were from six in the morning until six in the evening in the summer, and from seven in the morning until five in the winter. Their subjects were Greek, Latin, English grammar and spelling, manners, and public speaking. On top of it all they had catechism and daily prayers.

In spite of the long hours, the boys found time for fun and mischief. They had two hours off in the middle of the day, and in the summer there were long, light evenings for games and roughhouse. If they became too rough, or got into a fight, the headmaster took hold of their collars and separated them. He could even lay on the rod if necessary.

On Sunday the boys had to attend church, filing in orderly procession from the school to the nearby Anglican chapel.

William Penn did not see much of his parents or his young sister during his years at Chigwell, because school met all year round. There were just three short vacations: six days at Easter and at Pentecost and two weeks at Christmas time. But he liked school, and he liked his studies, and it soon became clear that he was a good scholar.

His personality deepened as he grew older. In between the times that he raced wildly around out-of-doors with the other students, there were moments when he was very thoughtful. When he reached ten or eleven he even showed signs of being religious.

One day he found himself sitting alone for a moment in one of the schoolrooms—alone and quiet—lost in thought. Suddenly he felt a deep inner peace and comfort. While he waited, almost without breathing, his inner feeling seemed like a glowing light, and the room seemed to grow bright.

"That must have been God," he whispered to himself. "That must have been God."

Not long after that, one of his father's menservants galloped up to the school leading a second saddle horse, and spoke a few hasty words to the headmaster. In another few minutes William Penn was mounted and galloping home to Wanstead.

"What is it?" he demanded.

The man was not permitted to tell him.

William found his mother supervising the packing of their things.

"Hurry!" she said the minute she saw him.

"Where are we going?"

"To London for a while."

"To our old house?"

"No; to temporary rooms on Tower Hill."

At last she told him. Cromwell had arrested his father. General Penn was in the Tower of London.

But his father was a national hero! How could Cromwell arrest him? And the Tower! People who were imprisoned in the Tower were usually put to death!

The ten miles to London seemed like ten thousand.

In London, the Penn family spent five weeks in an agony of worry and doubt. The day that General Penn was questioned before the Council of State, his wife and son simply walked about the house, walked about, walked about, and waited for news. When at last General Penn came to them, he did not stride through the door with his old zest.

"You are free!" gasped his wife.

He nodded. "Yes, free—and idle. I can no longer serve England while Cromwell is in power."

He was too crushed to say any more just then. But later he did try to explain the situation to his wife and son.

"My fleet had to transport army troops to the West Indies. We had orders to capture the island of Hispaniola from Spain. We suffered a terrible defeat."

"How can he arrest you for that?" Mrs. Penn asked.

"That was only Cromwell's excuse. He knows I am a Cavalier, loyal to my king. That is his real reason."

This was young William Penn's first taste of misfortune. Nothing had ever happened to upset his life before. His father had always come home with victories and promotions and triumphs at sea. He was just under eleven, but young though he was, he realized that this was a turning point in their lives.

The Penns returned to the Wanstead house for a few months, but William Penn did not go back to Chigwell School. Instead, he watched and waited while his parents planned to close up the Wanstead house.

"Where are we going?" he asked.

"We are going into exile, my son," his father told him. "We are going into exile in Ireland, until the tide shall turn."

On the 12th of August, 1656, they were all aboard ship, crossing St. George's Channel to Ireland. With them was a tutor for William, and Mrs. Penn carried her third child in her arms, the brand-new infant, Richard Penn.

CHAPTER TWO

Ireland

TO YOUNG PENN, Ireland was an adventure, in spite of the family misfortune. He'd never been to a foreign land before, and he stood at the ship's rail filled with excitement as the Irish coast came into view. It was just as his mother had described it to him: a deep, luscious green, because there was so much rainfall, and there were lovely hills and valleys, and the air was mild.

His mother stood beside him, and she laid a hand on his shoulder as she said, "Try to be calm, my son."

"Tell me about it," he demanded, talking very fast. "Will we go to the place where you were born?"

Mrs. Penn talked cheerfully, because she was glad to see Ireland again.

"My home was in the Dutch-English colony of Kilrush on the River Shannon," she told him. "That is on the western coast of Ireland. We are not going there. We are going to the village of Macroom on the River Lee in southern Ireland."

He was bursting with more questions.

"Our land in Kilrush is gone," she explained. "I lived there as a young girl, when I was Margaret Jasper; and I lived there as a young widow when my first husband, Nicasius Vanderschuren, died. But we were Protestant colonists, and the people of Ireland are Catholics. One day there was an armed uprising of the Irish Catholics, and we had to flee for our lives. That was when I came to London to live, and in London I met your father and married him."

His father appeared just then and said, "We must prepare to go ashore."

The vessel furled sail in the cove of Cork at the mouth of the River Lee, and the Penn family, with their belongings, traveled up the valley of the River Lee to Macroom. There, while General Penn was still in favor, Cromwell had granted him some lands as a reward for his services to England.

Macroom was an ancient village of small mud cottages with thatched roofs. At the edge of the village stood the castle, a square, gray-stone building, three stories tall. It had ample grounds and a high stone wall protecting the grounds. The Penns lived at the castle, and General Penn was in command of a foot company and troop of horse quartered there to protect the village. In case of attack the villagers took refuge inside the castle walls.

William Penn's seafaring father became a landed gentleman, home all the time. Father and son spent their days together, overseeing the peasants who planted and cultivated the land for them. William the younger learned how to manage an estate, and his father began to teach him how to handle a sword.

"You must be able to defend yourself," said his father. "Now, take hold of the sword thus."

William seized it, and rushed about, pointing it this way and that, stabbing imaginary foes.

"No! Wait, wait!" shouted his father. "You must not rush into it. You must pause—thus. Take your position—thus."

"Like this, Father?"

"That is fine."

"Then let us duel."

"No, no! You must learn patience and cunning. Study your opponent carefully. Learn his methods, his weaknesses."

"Why must it take so long?"

"Things that are well done take longer. You are too impetuous."

The Penns were in Ireland nearly four years, and during those years William learned a great deal. Most important of all, he learned how to be a colonist.

The castle and lands granted to the Penns had been taken away from an Irish family named MacCarthy. The English who received land grants in Ireland were really colonists. For generations England had been trying to subdue and conquer Ireland and settle the land with English Protestants. Oliver Cromwell had marched into Ireland with an army. By burning Irish cabins and cottages and destroying crops and cattle, he had managed to subdue part of Ireland for the time being.

The Penns wanted to return to London. They did not like the idleness of their life in Ireland and they were often lonely. But they were not completely cut off from their former life. Other English settlers took up land near them. Occasionally General Penn's naval friends put in at Cork harbor and brought him the latest political news.

William watched his father's face glow when he talked with his seafaring friends. He knew his father longed to stand once more with his feet on a rolling deck, shouting orders to the crew.

"Exiles never last forever," General Penn promised his son. "Some day the Stuart kings will be restored to the throne. Then we shall return to England, and you will go to a fine university."

William Penn went on studying with his tutor, preparing for the college days he hoped would come to pass. And, like the rest of his family, he went on longing for visits from occasional travelers to bring news from the outside world.

One day Macroom entertained a most extraordinary visitor. It all happened quite accidentally.

Word reached Macroom that there was a traveling preacher, named Thomas Loe, in the region.

"He speaks well," said one. "He draws large meetings."

"But he is a Quaker," said another.

General Penn nodded. He knew that the Quakers, or Friends, were a variety of Puritan, but he was a fairly open-minded man who was willing at times to listen to others. Perhaps this traveling fellow could liven up their days a bit.

"Let us be like the noble Bereans and invite him to speak to us here at Macroom," said General Penn.

Thomas Loe came to Macroom at once, and his visit caused a stir. A meeting gathered to hear him in one of the large rooms of the castle—the Penn family, the domestic staff, many of the troops and villagers.

William Penn, going on thirteen, sat down with the rest, feeling rather tense. How much was his father going to allow this Puritan-Quaker to say? Had it been a mistake to invite him? He hoped his father wouldn't grow angry, but he knew he could be quick-tempered.

Thomas Loe arose to speak. William Penn watched him. What a kindly and loving face the man had! Thomas Loe talked of feeling God's presence within oneself. He called it the Inner Light. It was a glow that one felt. A man or woman could meet with God any time anywhere, said Loe; he did not need a preacher or a church building.

Young Penn remembered the moment at Chigwell School when he had been sitting alone and had felt a glow and a light that he had known was God's presence.

Loe talked for a long time. Those who lived by the Inner Light, by God's love, he said, did not care for plumes and laces and fine silks. They preferred to be plain and simple. The Inner Light made a man want to be honest and humble and to live at peace with his fellow men. Those who lived by the Inner Light had no occasion for war.

William looked around the room. Everyone was deeply moved by Loe's words. A servant was weeping. There were even tears rolling down his father's cheeks!

Young Penn never forgot Thomas Loe's visit to Macroom. He never forgot Loe's message.

During the months that followed, political news continued to reach the Penns. The English navy was winning new victories at sea. The Puritans were becoming more divided among themselves . . . among the Puritans there were now Presbyterians, Baptists, Independents, Congregationalists, Quakers, and many more. They varied in their ideas from the most militant, like Cromwell, to the most gentle, like Thomas Loe.

The Puritan regime, the Penns heard, was still persecuting Church of England members. They seemed to forget that they themselves had once been persecuted and hadn't liked it. Because of the persecution, many Cavaliers or Royalists like General Penn were living in exile with their families.

But it was as General Penn had said, "Exiles never last forever." And a piece of political news threw the household into a turmoil of excitement.

"Oliver Cromwell is dead, General Penn! Cromwell is dead!"

"Did you hear that?" shouted the General. "His regime cannot last much longer! There's bound to be a turning!"

And there was a turning. Without the iron-handed Cromwell the Puritan rule soon collapsed, and political affairs in England fell into confusion.

In a few more months there was another piece of news for Macroom—a letter that General Penn waved happily in the air as he told his family what it said.

"A new parliament has been chosen!" he cried. "And I am to be one of its members."

He put an arm around his son's shoulders. They had grown very close during their years in Ireland.

"This new parliament will restore order in England once more," he told the fifteen-year-old William.

William was happy and excited because his father was. The tide had turned! They could all go back to England soon! They could go back to the city of London, back to good times, back to their own world. Great things awaited them all—a fine university, his father had promised him.

CHAPTER THREE

The Rest of Penn's Schooling

LONDON WAS ELECTRIC with politics! Young Penn wondered if he would ever feel calm again. He had arrived with his family in the month of March, 1660, and they had taken rooms on Tower Hill. He could see at once that his father was deep in the most important activities of the government. And his father shared much of it with him. General Penn would exchange a happy nod or a knowing wink with William, leap into his carriage and dash away—to a meeting of

Parliament, or a smaller meeting that he would explain later.

William knew what was going to happen. The King was to be restored to the throne.

During the first week of April, General Penn said to his family, "We are prepared to set sail!" and he glowed with happiness.

The entire English fleet—thirty-one ships—was ready to sail for Holland to bring home Charles II from exile. When the fleet left, General Penn was aboard the ship that would carry the King, and when it returned, young Penn was in the midst of the happy throngs that crowded the streets of London when the King reached the city. He watched the great triumph of men on horseback, men on foot, brandishing their swords and shouting with joy. The streets were strewn with flowers; the bells were ringing all over the city; buildings were hung with rich tapestries. At last, exhausted and spent from the experience, he returned home to wait for his father.

General Penn strode in triumphantly once more, and his family gathered around him, all talking at once, all begging for news—his wife Margaret, William, nine-year-old Margaret, and four-year-old Richard.

"The king has rewarded me for my help in restoring him to the throne," he told the loving circle. "As soon as he came aboard the ship in Holland, he laid his sword on my back and pronounced me a knight."

He would be Sir William from then on.

Sir William made his first-born son and heir a promise. "You will meet King Charles II, my son, and his brother James."

To be a courtier some day! That required education, and a gentlemanly polish.

"Oxford!" was Sir William's decision, and it was William's too.

Oxford University was one of England's most ancient seats of learning and one of the most dignified. Of its many colleges, Sir William chose Christ Church, and William was enrolled there on the 26th of October, 1660.

The change from home to college is always a big one. At home William Penn was surrounded by loving family and devoted servants. His four years in Ireland had been carefree, out-of-doors years, with a few short lessons a day from his tutor. Suddenly he found himself away from his family, obeying a strict schedule, and surrounded by crowds of rowdy young men.

He was deeply shocked by Oxford when he first arrived there. "It is a place of hellish darkness," he once said.

In all of the colleges of Oxford, there were 2,500 students, and at the college of Christ Church there were a hundred. Those 2,500 lads, turned loose at the end of the school day, raised plenty of commotion around town. They swarmed in and out of the taverns, divided themselves into warring factions, and fought it out in the streets. Or they banded together and fought it out with crowds of apprentices. Sometimes they roamed the streets at night singing lusty songs, or they gave riotous parties in their quarters.

Now that the Stuart kings had been restored to the throne, the rule of the Cavaliers and Royalists was being restored to England. All those who had been on Cromwell's side could expect trouble. There was nothing to stop the Oxford boys from beating up a Puritan, or ducking him in a pond. In fact, it was the newest fashion.

Gentleness came naturally to young Penn, and the classroom was more to his taste. There his Greek and Latin studies went on, and to them were added religion, philosophy, history, literature, and even a little law. His lessons were full of new challenges.

Christ Church was built in the shape of a rectangle with two-story buildings on all four sides and a grassy field in the center. The hundred students who attended Christ Church had their dormitories and their classrooms in those buildings. Just outside the rectangle stood Christ Church Cathedral where the students were required to worship.

The school year ran around the calendar, the way it had at Chigwell, with only short holidays such as Christmas and Easter. In the spring of Penn's first year at Oxford he had a special holiday—a very special opportunity to pay his family a visit—the Coronation. Eagerly he climbed into the carriage for the day-and-a-half drive to London.

His father greeted him with a lusty seaman's clap on the back. His mother hugged him and shed a few happy tears to notice how handsome and mature he was becoming.

"Your father has been appointed to a high post in the navy department," she bubbled over right away. "The King's brother James, Duke of York, is his superior. The Duke of York is Lord High Admiral."

"And your seat in Parliament?" William asked his father.

"I shall give that up and devote myself to naval affairs."

They chattered gaily together about the Coronation.

"We shall have a splendid view of the parade," said Sir William. "Mr. Young, the flagmaker, has a place in Cornhill, and he has invited us there. The procession will pass right under his windows."

Very early in the morning on Coronation Day, the Penns donned their finest clothes and drove to Cornhill. William went to Mr. Young's window and looked out. It would pass beneath them, right here, the most dazzling procession that London had ever seen. It would come from the Tower of London at the eastern end of the city and finish at the western end, in the section called Whitehall, where many government buildings stood. How gay Cornhill looked! It was decorated with great archways of flowers, and the fronts of the buildings were hung with bright silks and tapestries. And the crowds were growing thicker and thicker.

"Here it comes!" went up the shout.

Men on foot and horseback, dressed in velvet, gold, silver, jewels, rich embroidery—marching proudly!

One of Mr. Young's guests was so dazzled he had to turn his eyes away.

"It is impossible to relate the glory of this day," he gasped.

William Penn could not turn away. He simply gazed and gazed while his heart beat wildly. *His* father was part of this. *His* father was on intimate terms with the most important men in the procession. And he was part of his father's life.

The most thrilling moment of all occurred when the King and the Duke of York passed beneath Mr. Young's windows. The King must have known where the Penns would be, because he looked right up at them and paid them a nod and smile. Father and son bowed deeply.

"Did you see that?" cried Sir William, and hugged his son.

William had seen. He felt as though he were going to suffocate.

When the parade finally passed, they all took dinner with Mr. Young, and William sat beside his father, listening to the conversation, much of it about the inner workings of the government, especially the navy department.

Penn returned to Oxford feeling years older. He was almost seventeen, a very mature age for those times. By now he was very much at home among the Oxford men.

The glow of the Coronation wore off slowly but surely, and the effect of having the Stuart king back in power began to show. Persecution of the Puritan sects was growing crueler and crueler. Laws were passed by the Cavalier Parliament to help the persecution along. Anyone who did not worship in the Church of England was breaking the law. Everyone must conform or suffer terrible consequences.

As William Penn walked through the streets of Oxford town, he saw Puritans in the stocks being pelted with stones, or he watched Quakers being dragged off to prison. Such sights made him reflect and wonder.

When he thought about John Fell, the Dean of Christ Church, he wondered still more. Dr. Fell was a devoted Royalist, and he went joyfully about his task of making the students of Christ Church conform. Every student must wear a surplice, or long student's gown. Every student must worship God in the Christ Church Cathedral. Why?—Penn asked himself. Why must everyone be exactly alike, or pretend to be? Most of the students were Cavaliers or Royalists, but not all. Some were Puritans. The Puritans were serious and studious lads; so was William Penn. They were gentle and more kindly than the Royalists; so was William Penn. He began to make friends with them.

"John Fell was not always our dean," one of them told him. "We had a wonderful dean, Dr. John Owen. But he was a non-conformist. When the monarchy was restored he was dismissed and Dr. Fell was appointed in his place."

William Penn wanted to hear more about Dr. Owen.

"Would you like to hear him speak?" one of the students asked. "His home is right here in Oxford town."

Eagerly Penn nodded. He went with the non-conformist students to hear Dr. John Owen. Owen proved to be a brilliant and sincere man. Penn respected him deeply. "My own beliefs and ideas are gradually changing," Penn began to realize. Many of the ideas that Dr. Owen taught the young men reminded Penn of the things Thomas Loe had said on his visit to Macroom Castle in Ireland.

Thomas Loe and John Owen were right. Men were individuals. No two were alike. Each man must make his own decisions—about life, about God, about practically everything.

The more severe Dean Fell became with the students, the more rebellious the Puritans grew. They refused to wear the surplice. They refused to attend Anglican church services, and even held their own worship meetings separately. William Penn was among them. He turned his back on what he called "black tribes of scholars" who were so cruel and thoughtless, and found his companions among the quieter, more dignified group who followed Dr. Owen.

Dean Fell and the rest of the faculty took measures to bring the rebellion to an end. Some had to pay fines; others were expelled. Since William Penn's father was a close personal friend of the King and the Duke of York, the faculty was more patient with him. First they made him pay a fine, but he still did not conform. He went right on attending Dr. Owen's lectures and staying away from Anglican services. At last, Dean Fell's patience gave out, and William Penn was expelled from college.

He knew the news would reach his father before he could reach home himself. And he knew his father's disposition. As a high-ranking naval officer Sir William was used to commanding other men. He was used to obedience. He had a quick temper and a strong hand.

The whipping that he expected was waiting for him. It was a painful and difficult time for the whole family. Lady Penn wept and wrung her hands, as she watched her husband thrash her son. As a final gesture he took William by the collar and started for the door.

"I shall turn you out of the house! You have brought disgrace on us all!"

His mother rushed to interfere.

"He's your son!" she reminded Sir William. "Where can the boy go if you turn him out? How can he live? What can he do but go straight to the Puritans? How can we protect him from them if he isn't here in the house?"

William was too proud to say anything.

"I need him when you're away at sea!" Lady Penn pleaded.

And it was true. William was the oldest. He was head of the house and protector of the family when his father was away. Sir William let go of his collar.

"Very well," said Sir William. "You may remain."

Relations were badly strained around the house after that. William kept to his room a great deal. He felt alone, and he needed comforting advice. To whom could he talk? Not his father. His mother? No. She did not really understand the question of non-conformity. Then he had it. He would write to Dr. Owen. William Penn began to exchange letters with him, and Dr. Owen's letters gave him courage.

One day his father came to William's room with a piece of paper in his hand.

"Is this yours?" he asked.

William's heart sank. It was one of Dr. Owen's letters. He expected another violent scene. But not this time. Sir William had begun to realize how seriously his son was involved with the Puritans and that a thrashing would do no good.

"I have discussed this with some of my friends in the Government, son William," the older man began. "They have made many suggestions. I think the best is to send you to school in France for a while."

William nodded to his father. He realized that he needed the experience of traveling and studying in Europe if he was to be a courtier. Every young gentleman of the times was supposed to have a trip through Europe to complete his education.

"Some persons of quality are leaving soon," his father added. "You can go as far as Paris with them. I can arrange to have you visit the Royal Court of France, too. After that you will study at the Protestant Academy of Saumur."

William Penn had a gay, adventuresome side as well as a serious side. To travel abroad, to a new and foreign country, without his father! His pulse began to race and his eyes sparkled. Sir William smiled with relief to see it.

"I shall learn to speak French, Father!"

"Learn as much as you can, my son."

Young Penn had come home from Oxford in March. Early in July he was packed and on his way to France.

Paris turned out to be a gay city, and, just as his father had hoped, Penn did forget the Puritans for a while. He became completely absorbed by what he saw and the people he met. Louis XIV was King of France, and he was a young man who liked to wear satins and laces, eat rich foods, drink fine wines, and have gay parties at his court. He set the fashions for everybody who could afford to imitate him. Penn saw ladies and gentlemen, dressed like peacocks, strolling through the Tuileries Gardens in Paris. He tasted new wines. He dined at parties where the meat was cut in thin slices instead of being served in great joints the way it was in England.

He soon learned that manners and etiquette were extremely complicated in France, and that the French considered fine manners highly important. William Penn had to be careful of every word and remember to pay due respect to every person of rank.

One night Penn was returning through the streets of Paris to his lodgings, when suddenly he found himself challenged to a sword duel by a stranger.

"I doffed my hat to you, and you did not return the courtesy," said the man.

It did Penn no good to say, "I saw you not."

He had to whip out his sword and defend his life. Penn was an expert swordsman by then, and he soon had the man disarmed and on the ground. Under French law he was entitled to kill the man, but something stopped him.

Kill a man for a hat? No. He could not.

"Arise and go your way," he told the man. "The doffing of a hat is not worth a man's life."

William Penn did not remain in Paris very long. After a visit to the Royal Court at nearby Fontainebleau, he set out for Saumur.

Saumur is in the rolling, meadowy countryside of southwestern France, on the southern bank of the Loire River. This was the heart of the chateau country, and Saumur had its chateau, or castle, perched on top of a hill in the center of the town. The castle is there today, and so is the school building at 6 Rue St. Jean, and many other houses of Penn's time.

Moses Amyraut was the principal or headmaster of the Protestant Academy of Saumur, and he was one of the greatest religious teachers of his times.

Sitting in the classroom, listening to Moses Amyraut, William Penn felt his serious side awaken once more. He remembered the ideas he had learned from the Puritans and from Thomas Loe. He forgot the gay parties of Paris.

Moses Amyraut thrilled him. Amyraut taught freedom and toleration. A man had to be free in order to be good, he said, and being good meant nothing unless it was voluntary. A man had to obey his conscience, and his conscience had to be guided by God's spirit. Worshiping God was not enough, though, said Moses Amyraut. A good man had to think of his fellow man. He had to be ready to help his fellow man whenever help was needed.

William Penn was even fortunate enough to live at Dr. Amyraut's home. Many of the poorer students had to manage as best they could around town in the inns and cheap boarding houses.

He took other subjects at Saumur—Greek, grammar, public speaking, mathematics—but nothing meant as much to him as the ideas of Moses Amyraut.

After spending about two years in France, Penn returned to London in the summer of 1664. Those two years had made a big change in him. He had much more poise. He spoke excellent French and dressed in the latest fashions.

Sir William put his hands on his son's shoulders and held him at arm's length. What a splendid man his son had grown to be! He could hold his own in a conversation with the most important men at court. Lady Penn beamed happily at the handsome young man. To his thirteen-year-old sister Margaret and nine-year-old brother Richard he was completely a man of the world.

"Now!" declared his father joyfully. "Your education needs one more touch: law."

If William was to follow in his father's footsteps,

then certainly some legal training would come in handy.

There were four law schools in London called the Inns of Court. They were for young men of wealth and "quality." William Penn enrolled in Lincoln's Inn on February 7, 1665.

Once more he found himself amongst arrogant, fun-loving, and spoiled young men. They spent more time at their celebrations than at their studies. But he was not as shocked as he had been at Oxford when he was only sixteen. At Lincoln's Inn he was almost twenty-one.

He joined the other young men in the Old Hall where they spent most of their time. The Old Hall was nearly seventy-five feet long and its ceiling thirty feet high. The walls inside were of dark oak and the tall, narrow windows were stained glass. The floor was tile, and covered with rushes. In the center of the floor a fire burned and sent its smoke up to the ceiling, where it escaped through vents at the joining of the side walls and ceiling. There, in the Old Hall, the law students dined at long tables or gave plays and held mock trials.

Penn began to enjoy his law studies. This was useful knowledge. He was a skillful talker by now, and there was much in English law that deserved to be talked about.

In a few weeks his father called him home. England had declared war against Holland, and the fleet was going into action. Sir William Penn was Great Captain Commander of one of its three squadrons.

William thought his father wanted to give him instructions about family affairs. He was startled to hear his father say, "I am taking you with me."

"Into combat?"

"No. You will be with me only briefly."

His father's ship was the *Royal Charles.* As William Penn walked her decks he could look up into the billowing sails or see at a distance the other ships of the fleet, dipping their bows into the waves. He could watch his father commanding more than eight thousand men. The men loved and trusted Sir William. What a splendid commander his father was!

William Penn was aboard for nearly three weeks before he was at last called to his father's cabin for an explanation.

"I am sending you home, Son William, as my personal messenger to the King."

So that was it! That was how his father was arranging his meeting with the King. King Charles would of course have to receive the personal messenger of one of his top commanders.

William Penn went aboard a smaller ship bound for Harwich. From there he went straight up to London and to Whitehall, arriving at the palace at dawn. The King was not yet up, he was told.

"Please tell His Majesty that it is a messenger from the *Royal Charles.*"

He was soon ushered in, and he found that the King had gotten out of bed and donned robe and slippers.

"Oh, is't you?" the King remarked with surprise. "And how is Sir William?"

William Penn delivered his packet of letters and remained with the King as long as he dared. Later, he wrote his father a long letter describing the interview.

And so back to Lincoln's Inn once more, but not for long. In another few weeks his law studies were interrupted again.

An epidemic of the plague had begun to spread in London. There were usually some cases of the dreaded disease among the poorest people, and so no one felt alarmed at a few cases during the winter and spring. But when the weather turned hot, the number began to increase. By July London was in a panic. The stricken were dying so fast they had to be gathered in wagons and taken to big graves. More and more houses were boarded up. Bonfires were burned in the streets to purify the air. Everyone who could afford a wagon or carriage loaded his belongings into it and fled to the open countryside. Lincoln's Inn closed its doors and sent its students home to their families.

The Penns did not leave London, and none of them caught the illness either. But it had a deep effect on William Penn just the same. He had never seen so much human suffering before. To make matters worse the authorities went right on persecuting the Puritan sects. During the summer months, when plague victims were dying so fast they fell right in the street, victims of persecution stood in the stocks for their beliefs. Penn watched while the Quakers, in spite of the danger of being arrested, came out to help the sick. They nursed the afflicted; they carried food to houses that were quarantined.

One elderly Quaker said lightheartedly, "I always carry my nightcap in my pocket. Then if I am arrested my head will be warm in prison."

William Penn remembered the teaching of Moses Amyraut. Worshiping God was not enough, Amyraut had said. A man had to be ready to help his fellow man whenever help was needed.

CHAPTER FOUR

The Tower of London

THE PLAGUE SUBSIDED in the autumn, and London life became normal again. William Penn and the other young men went back to their law studies.

Sir William came home from the Dutch war, triumphant once more. But his family could see that he was growing old. One foot was painfully swollen with the gout, and he had to sit in a chair with his foot up on a cushion for a while.

"I feel deeply grateful that I have so capable a son

to take over my affairs," he said with deep feeling.

William sat with him, going over details. There was one thing he must do for his father. He must go to Ireland to straighten out property matters there.

King Charles had asked Sir William to exchange his Macroom lands for other lands in Ireland. The King wanted to give Macroom back to the original Irish owners, the MacCarthys, from whom it had been seized by Cromwell. Sir William had of course consented. He would do anything for his king.

Father and son agreed that William should give up his law studies and go to Ireland for a while instead. William was soon on his way, traveling across England by coach and then across St. George's Channel to the port of Kinsale in a small sailing vessel.

He looked happily at the rich green coastline of Ireland, where the grasses and trees grew right to the water's edge. His destination this time was the tiny Irish village of Shanagarry, a handful of cabins dotted along the road. Shanagarry Village was just a few miles north of Cork Harbor. Close to the village, within a short walk of the sea, was Shanagarry Castle. The castle, built of the native gray stone, now belonged to his father—along with more than seven thousand acres.

Penn lived at the castle while he was in Ireland.

He set to work at once—talking to the farmers who rented portions of the land, straightening out boundary lines between tenants, issuing new leases, collecting rents.

There was zest in the work. He enjoyed overseeing

the tenants and looking after such a big tract of land.

Once in a while he went up to Dublin, where his father's land claim had to be heard before the land commissioners. There was a royal court in Dublin, like the one in London, only smaller. There he met the noblemen and gentry of Ireland. Once the men stationed in the garrison of Carrickfergus mutinied, and William Penn served under the Earl of Arran in restoring order. He cut a gallant figure in his armor, handling both musket and sword with a great flourish.

But Cork was the city nearest to Shanagarry, and Penn rode to Cork oftener than to Dublin. He went to Cork one day to buy some clothes. Which shop? he pondered as he jogged through one of the streets. He remembered that a Quaker had a shop somewhere in town, and the Quakers were known to be honest shopkeepers. He had been in the shop with his father when they were living at Macroom. This day he dismounted and strode into the store once more.

"Good day," he said.

"Good day to thee," said the woman behind the counter, and she smiled cordially.

Penn remembered her, but she did not recognize the tall, handsome cavalier. He had been only a stripling boy on his last visit.

He stood chatting with her for several minutes. There was no hurry about the purchase.

"I know many of the Friends or Quakers," he told her, and then he asked, "Do you know a man named Thomas Loe?" Her face lighted up happily, and she nodded.

Penn told her how his father had invited Thomas Loe to speak to the household at Macroom.

"I'd walk a hundred miles to hear Thomas Loe speak again!" he said enthusiastically.

"Thou needst not walk so far, Friend. Thomas Loe is right here in Cork, and he will be speaking to a Quaker meeting tomorrow evening."

Penn gazed at her as though he didn't quite believe what he heard.

"Remain over in Cork until tomorrow, Friend William Penn. Thou art welcome at my home, or the home of any Quaker in Cork for that matter."

William Penn did remain over with the Friends.

For the first time in his life he felt self-conscious about his expensive clothing, his lace-ruffled cuffs, the big feather plume in his hat, his elegant wig and clanking sword. The Quakers dressed plainly—no laces, no plumes, no swords. And they spoke plainly, too, using the familiar thee and thou instead of the plural you which was considered a more polite form. The Quakers believed that all men are equal, and so they used the language of the commonest people no matter to whom they were speaking.

When William Penn went into the Friends' meeting the next evening and sat down amongst them, he felt deeply excited and very curious. Thomas Loe had once made his father weep. Would the same thing happen to himself tonight?

The meeting settled into silence and sat very still. At last a member arose to speak, but Penn was not very impressed with what the man said. More silence. Another member arose, and when he turned around to face the meeting, Penn recognized Thomas Loe. Loe looked much older. He had probably been working and traveling hard.

"There is a faith that overcometh the world," Thomas Loe began.

Twenty-two-year-old Penn listened more and more intently as Thomas Loe spoke on. Loe reminded him of all his religious experiences and all of his disturbing thoughts. He remembered what Loe had once said at Macroom about the Inner Light that made a man want to be honest and humble and peaceable. He remembered his Puritan classmates at Oxford, and Dr. John Owen. He remembered the teachings of Moses Amyraut in France. He remembered how the Quakers had come out to nurse the sick during the epidemic of plague in London. It all swept over him like an ocean wave.

Thomas Loe finished and sat down. William Penn felt that he must speak, *must* speak, and he rose in place. But he could not produce a single word. His voice was choked with tears. All he could do was stand and weep and hope that his tears would tell Loe and the Quakers how he felt.

He had been reached by the Quaker message. He knew it. The Friends knew it. As soon as the meeting was over, they crowded around Penn lovingly, and again he went home with some of them to spend the night. In fact, he stayed at the same home as Thomas Loe. He and Loe had a long talk together.

From then on William Penn hurried eagerly to attend the Quaker meetings in Ireland. Since they were just as persecuted in Ireland as in England, he was soon in trouble.

The soldiers liked to harass the meetings and disturb them when they had a chance. Penn was sitting in a meeting one day when a rough soldier came stomping and shouting in. Impetuously, Penn leaped from his seat, picked the ruffian up by the collar, and started with him toward the head of a flight of stairs. The Quakers rushed to interfere.

"No, no!" they protested. "Violence is not our way. Let the man go."

As soon as Penn realized what he had done, he was embarrassed by his own impatience. But the damage was done. The soldier went off in a huff, gathered a few companions, and came back and arrested the whole meeting. They were brought before the Mayor of Cork.

As soon as the Mayor noticed Penn's fancy clothing, he said, "You must have been arrested in error. You are free to go."

That was the moment when William Penn made his great decision—to join the Society of Friends.

"I am a Friend," he told the Mayor. "My arrest was not a mistake, and I wish to be treated the same as the others."

He did more than that. He stepped forward and became the lawyer of the group of prisoners.

"With what crime are we charged?" he demanded.

"Being present at a tumultuous and riotous assembly, and further, unless you give bond for your good behavior you will all be committed to prison."

Penn argued the case carefully, as he had learned to do at Lincoln's Inn, pointing out that there was really no law which applied. There had been no riot. The charge was false. It did no good. The whole group was taken to Cork prison.

At the door of the prison, Penn paused. There was one thing more. These were peaceable people. They were opposed to fighting and violence. If he joined them he must do things their way. With a cavalier's flourish he unbuckled his sword and handed it to a bystander.

"Take my sword," he said. "I shall need it no longer."

Scarcely had the prison door clanged shut than Penn wrote to the Earl of Orrery, Lord President of Munster. Munster is a province of Ireland made up of six counties including County Cork.

"Religion, which is at once my crime and mine innocence, makes me a prisoner to a mayor's malice," he wrote. He told the Earl of Orrery that the Friends were unjustly imprisoned. They were not a tumultuous people. They had simply met to worship God in their own way.

The Penn name carried as much weight in Ireland as it did in England. The Penns were personal friends of the ruling family. In a very short time the Quakers were released from prison.

But others were writing letters—to Sir William in London—warning him that his son was in bad company in Ireland. Sir William wrote one of his own:

Navy Office, October 12, 1667

SON WILLIAM:

I have writ several letters to you since I received any from you. By this I charge you and strictly command that you come to me with all possible speed. In expectation of your compliance, I remain

Your affectionate father,
W. PENN

William Penn had to obey his father, even though he did not want to leave Ireland just when he was beginning to feel at home there.

"There are Quaker meetings in London," his new friends reminded him.

"I am going to London," said Josiah Coale, a Quaker minister who was older than Penn. "I shall travel with thee and talk to thy father with thee."

Penn and Coale set out, and when they reached London they found the city charred and ruined. The Great Fire had swept over it, burning through the wooden buildings for four days and four nights, helped along by a high wind. The fire had begun in a baker's shop on Pudding Lane near the London Bridge, and before anyone realized it was serious it was sweeping westward across the city. Thirteen thousand houses vanished. Penn and Coale rode past acres of ruin that bristled with stone pillars and solitary walls. Some new buildings were going up, but many Londoners were living in tents or lean-tos fashioned out of the rubble.

Sir William had moved his family from the ruined city to a house in Wanstead, Essex County, another big place richly furnished with tapestries, needlework chairs, feather beds, silk and satin quilts, and heavy curtains. Josiah Coale drove out to Wanstead with William Penn, and that did soften the first meeting of father and son. Sir William held his temper in front of the visitor, even when his own son addressed him as *thee* and *thou,* and even when his son and Josiah Coale kept their hats on in the house. But once Coale had gone upstairs for the night, Sir William burst forth.

"What is the idea of addressing me as *thee* and *thou?*"

"I am obeying God's will," said William, "and I mean no disrespect to thee."

"Do you not realize how important it is to use the plural *you* when speaking to someone older or of higher rank? I've given you an excellent upbringing. Does that mean nothing?"

Quakers recognized no rank, William explained. They considered all men equal.

"Surely, when you address the King, the Duke of York, and me, I can expect you to use the polite form."

William shook his head. "I am sorry, Father."

"And remove your hat!"

William did not. The Friends uncovered to no man, neither did they bend the knee.

His father was so beside himself with rage that they

did not dare talk any more that night. How could a son of his have joined the Quakers?

"Be prepared to go out with me in the coach in the morning," was his father's last order.

William went upstairs to his room, but he couldn't sleep. He loved his father, and he could not hurt his father without hurting himself. He wondered what would happen in the morning, and he discovered quickly enough.

Since it was extremely dangerous politically to be a non-conformist, his father wanted to drive out into the park where they could talk without being overheard.

"Son William," the father began, "I have trained you up in learning and other accomplishments for a courtier—as for an ambassador or other minister. How, in the face of that, can you become a Quaker?"

" 'Tis in obedience to the voice of God in my own conscience."

They talked and talked and got nowhere.

"You would give up the life and career I have won for you?"

"Yes, Father.

Relations were strained at the Wanstead house after that. William spent most of his time with the Quakers in London.

"William Penn has such zeal, such energy!" they said. "He is fast becoming one of our best ministers."

The Friends had no paid ministers. By minister they really meant spiritual leader, or any member who showed more talent than others for speaking in meeting for worship. Once Penn had rediscovered his tongue, he became as eloquent a speaker for Quakerism as he ever had been in law school or court circles. Because he had such a fine education, his words were rich and poetical and full of Bible phrases. He called God the "everlasting arm of strength," and declared, "let the winds of imagination blow, the storms of persecution beat, and the sea of raging malice foam . . . we shall still confide and rejoice in the everlasting God."

Tattlers kept Sir William up-to-date on his son's activities, and soon there was another family scene. Sir William's health was failing; William was his heir. Government in high places was full of intrigue. Could not William realize how dangerous and embarrassing his Quaker associations were? Quakers were the hated sect, the most extreme of all the Puritans! But William would not yield. In desperation Sir William told him to pack his clothes and leave the house for good.

It was a tragic day for the Penn family, and Lady Penn's pleadings did no good this time.

Left without any means of support, William went straight up to London—to the Friends. He flung himself into the work of the Quaker movement. It became his single interest in life. Full of ardor and energy, he hurried from task to task. He appeared in public debates. He wrote tracts and pamphlets.

His first tract, *Truth Exalted,* did not stir up much attention. It was very short and written in too much of a hurry. But he soon produced another, *The Sandy*

Foundation Shaken. In it he denied and refuted many of the beliefs of the Church of England. A storm arose around him at once. In a matter of days the Principal Secretary of State issued a warrant for his arrest.

"I shall not resist you," he told the constable who came to arrest him.

If prison was the service God wanted of him, then prison it must be.

He was placed in the Tower of London, in a tiny room under the roof. As he sat down in his new quarters, he felt the cold and chill of the winter day slowly penetrating his being, and he wrapped his cloak more tightly around himself.

"No visitors," he was told, "unless they have special permission of the authorities."

Soon he was up and trying to walk around in the cramped space. He was a man of action! He wanted to be about and doing things? No, he must be patient. He must await God's will. He sat down again.

In a few days his personal manservant appeared at the prison door, bringing a message from the Bishop of London: "You may recant in the public market place before all the city or else be a prisoner for the rest of your life."

Penn needed no time to think of his answer: "My prison shall be my grave before I will budge a jot, for I owe my conscience to no mortal man."

He was left alone for a long time after that. His only visitor was the attendant who brought him the terrible prison food. He was not even allowed to have a barber.

"May I have permission to move about in the yard for exercise?" he asked.

"No!" came back the answer.

There were many important men in the government who loved and respected Sir William, and for his sake they tried to help his son. In a few weeks the King sent his own personal chaplain to the Tower to see Penn. The chaplain, Dr. Edward Stillingfleete, was a young and enthusiastic fellow like the prisoner.

"The Tower is the worst argument in the world to convince me," William Penn said to Dr. Stillingfleete.

The excitable, impatient young Penn had to discipline himself to be calm and patient. Self-discipline grew easier for him over the years, but this first real test was hard. He decided to concentrate on writing. He first wrote a tract, or short book, called *No Cross, No Crown.* In it he explained several Quaker principles: why Quakers did not remove their hats as a gesture of respect, why they dressed plainly, why they said *thee* and *thou.* Writing about these things made them clearer in his own mind.

Quakerism was fairly new. The movement had been started by George Fox when William Penn was about three years old. George Fox was the son of a weaver, and he had been born in Fenny Drayton, Leicestershire. As soon as he was old enough, his father apprenticed him to a shoemaker. But George Fox was a disturbed and discontented young man, who did not know what he wanted to do with his life. His parents were Puritans and deeply religious, and as he grew up, he became more and more interested in religion, and less and less interested in shoemaking. But the churches that he knew didn't satisfy him. At last, when he was nineteen, George Fox left home and began to travel about England, trying to find the kind of church he would be happy in. He talked with teachers and preachers, about religion, about the Bible. He prayed and fasted. He traveled on.

Since he was not the son of a gentleman, he had only a modest education. But of what use was great learning, he wondered, if it did not bring a man closer to God? Why not become a soldier? someone suggested. George Fox shuddered at the idea. He saw people going into churches and cathedrals to worship. They didn't need their church buildings, he decided. God was everywhere.

After three years of searching and wandering, George Fox found his answer. Here is how he described it in his *Journal:* "But as I had forsaken all the priests, so I left the separate preachers also, and those called the most experienced people; for I saw there was none among them all that could speak to my condition. And when all my hopes in them and in all men were gone, so that I had nothing outwardly to help me, nor could tell what to do, then, Oh then, I heard a voice which said, 'There is one, even Christ Jesus, that can speak to thy condition,' and when I heard it my heart did leap for joy."

That was it! God dwelt in every man. Man could

talk with God directly any time anywhere. It was only necessary to wait in silence—the silence of the heart and mind—and let the Inner Light grow bright. The Inner Light would guide the individual on the right path.

Joyfully George Fox traveled on—all over England—telling anyone who would listen about his new discovery. Many others had been as discontented as he, and they listened. Of course he made the authorities angry. Sometimes he was beaten, other times he was thrown into prison. He was a strong, sturdy man. He kept on with his preaching until he had a large following, and this group soon became known as the Society of Friends. Fox called them his "Children of Light."

We don't know exactly when William Penn first met George Fox. But when Penn was placed in the Tower of London, he had probably not yet met Fox. He knew *about* Fox, though, and he understood clearly what Fox believed. He believed it, too. That was why he had joined the Society of Friends. And that was why he was now in prison.

William Penn longed deeply to make his father understand why he had joined the Friends or Quakers. He knew his father was suffering from this experience. So, the next thing that he wrote in the Tower was a long letter to Sir William, explaining his new religious ideas.

It helped a little, for his father actually came to the Tower himself to see William. The two men loved each other deeply, even though a quarrel was dividing them.

"They say that in your tract, *Sandy Foundation,* you deny Christ, my son."

"They lie who say that! The tract was not intended to deny Christ."

After a strained and painful conversation, Sir William returned home and sent a petition to the King's Privy Council, asking for his son's release. No release came. The prisoner himself wrote to the Principal Secretary of State.

The weeks passed and the weather grew hot. The tiny attic room became as suffocating as an oven from the summer sun. The little bit of hair that had grown back on Penn's head since he had had the smallpox fell away from neglect.

At last Dr. Stillingfleete came to see William Penn again, and they held a long conversation together, trying to find some solution. Suddenly Dr. Stillingfleete hit upon an idea.

"Your enemies claim that your tract denies Christ," he said. "You say you believe in Christ. I believe you. Now, why not write another tract explaining your exact views and send it to the King and Council?"

Of course! Penn sat about the task immediately. In a few days he had completed *Innocency with Her Open Face.* He sent it off to Whitehall, and it turned out to be a very wise move.

The King met with his Council on July 28, 1669. Together they considered William Penn's second tract and Dr. Stillingfleete's opinion. They nodded their heads. The prisoner was to be set free and delivered to the custody of his father.

Nearly nine months in that uncomfortable attic room! A real test of courage and faith!

There remained one more test: the return home. Slowly, thoughtfully, he jogged along the road to Wanstead, and with a beating heart he entered the door. He could see the unhappiness in his father's face. But by now Sir William understood that William was determined to make his own way in the world. He held out his hand.

"Sit down with me, Son William."

They felt very self-conscious with one another, but at least they were able to discuss plans.

"You have suffered so much notoriety because of your imprisonment," said Sir William, "that I think it would be best for you to leave the country for a while. I am sending you back to Ireland."

William nodded agreement, but he looked at the floor. He could not tell his father that there was still something else on his mind, something to make the Irish exile harder. No; he would not tell Sir William. He had caused Sir William sufficient suffering for the time being.

CHAPTER FIVE

Newgate Prison

WILLIAM PENN SET OUT on horseback one morning soon after his talk with his father. He took the road leading due west to Bristol. His pace was rather slow for a man who usually rushed into everything he did. But scarcely was he out of London than he turned his horse's head into a road going in a northwesterly direction. His pace quickened; a smile appeared on his lips. Bristol was not ahead of him, he knew, but the village of Amersham in Buckingham County was.

Buckinghamshire is beautiful countryside with dales and hills and roads winding through tall, gray beech trees. Penn reached Amersham on the second day, and he soon saw the house where he wanted to visit—Bury Farm, home of the Peningtons.

Isaac and Mary Penington were Quakers. They had once been wealthy, but their big home and much of their money had been confiscated when they joined the sect. When that happened, they simply moved to Bury Farm and went right on working in the movement.

The Peningtons were a large family, and they were overjoyed to see William Penn come walking through the door.

"Stay with us a day or two, Friend William."

He knew they would say that, and he did spend several happy days with them. He sat with them at their big dinner table; he went to meeting with them. And Mary and Isaac Penington smiled happily, because they knew why he had come. He had come to see the oldest of their children, Gulielma Springett.

Gulielma Springett was Mary Penington's daughter by a former marriage. She was the same age as William Penn, and she was a quiet, gentle, sensitive type of person. Those who met her for the first time were always startled by her beauty.

William Penn had met her about a year before, in the home of some London Friends. She had come into the room while he was there, and they had been introduced. They clasped hands after the manner of

Friends. A few minutes later she had left, and that was all. For Penn that was enough. He never forgot Gulielma Springett. All during his long months in the Tower, she had been on his mind. Three weeks after his release from prison, he started out for Bristol where he was to take a boat to Ireland. Only, he took a very unusual route to Bristol—through Amersham.

During his visit with the Peningtons he and Gulielma spent as much time together as they could.

"I know not how long I shall be in Ireland," he told her.

"I shall miss thee, William, and be here to greet thee when thou returnest."

"We can write to each other."

He tarried with the Peningtons and Gulielma Springett as long as he dared. But at last he had to take his leave of them.

When he set out from Amersham, he had two new traveling companions: Guli's half-brother, the fourteen-year-old John Penington, and Philip Ford. Penn had engaged Philip Ford as his personal secretary and steward. Ford was a Quaker merchant, but his business wasn't doing well, and he decided to accept the position as Penn's aide.

When Penn, Ford, and young Penington reached Bristol, there was another delay. They had to wait for a boat to take them to Ireland.

It proved almost as happy a delay as the one at Amersham. For in Bristol Penn had ample opportunity to become acquainted with George Fox. George

Fox was planning to be married to Margaret Fell, and Penn arrived in the midst of the preparations for the wedding. Margaret Fell was from the northern part of England, and she had done so much work in the Society of Friends that she was called the "mother of Quakerism."

Penn and his two companions finally set sail for Ireland.

Penn thought his heart would burst with grief at what he heard as soon as he reached the city of Cork. Persecution of the Quakers had intensified. Scores of them were in prison. He hurried to the Cork prison. There he saw children in stocks, eighty Friends in one small enclosure with no food or drink except what could be pushed through a hole. Servants were in the stocks who had run the risk of bringing food, bedding, and tools of trade.

"This is English abusing English! This is Protestant persecuting Protestant! How can such things go on?" he cried.

And there were more Friends in Dublin prison, he was told.

William Penn went to work at once. He was a man who could work long, hard hours and get along on very little sleep. He had Philip Ford to help him, as well as the Quakers who were not in prison. True enough, he was there to look after his father's lands, but that could be fitted in somehow. His first big task was to obtain the freedom of the Quakers.

He had one great advantage that none of the other

Friends had. That was his influence with the government. Since England ruled Ireland, the government men were chosen by Charles II. They knew how close Penn's father and the King were.

He traveled back and forth between Dublin and Cork. He wrote to the Mayor of Cork. He went personally to see the Mayor of Dublin, carrying a written petition from Friends.

"You Quakers should be lashed out of town," said the Mayor of Dublin, and with a sneer he threw the paper to the ground.

Penn wrote to such members of the Irish nobility as the Earl of Drogheda, the Earl of Arran, the Earl of Roscommon. He and other Quakers composed a letter to the Lord Lieutenant of Ireland, and with the Lord Lieutenant's help they petitioned the Council. In a few more days, Penn the diplomat was triumphant. The Quakers in the Dublin prison went free.

"Now to the Friends in Cork!" declared the energetic Penn.

All the while he was working for the imprisoned Quakers he was attending to a great many other matters. He traveled around Ireland visiting out-of-the-way Friends' meetings. He looked after his father's lands. He wrote letters home. He wrote to his father about property matters, to his sister Margaret who was married by now to Anthony Lowther and living in northern England, and he wrote often to Gulielma Springett.

Regarding the Friends in Cork prison, he wrote to

Lord Shannon and Lord Barrymore, and again to the Lord Lieutenant of Ireland. He even gave an elaborate banquet for some of the Irish nobility. The Irish nobility learned to like him so well that some of them even came to Quaker meetings so that they could hear him preach.

At last he was admitted to a private session with the Lord Lieutenant, and he soon came rushing back to his friends, happy and out of breath:

"He promised to release Friends and did so by order of Council in the afternoon."

With so much accomplished in Ireland, he began to feel restless. He wanted to return to Gulielma. When a letter came from his father asking him to come home, he was overjoyed. There was a command he was happy to obey.

As soon as he reached the Wanstead house, William Penn realized why his father had sent for him. The snappy old sea dog had lost his snap. He was very ill. Sir William had what his doctor called "dropsy scurvey and jaundice." He could manage to stroll in his garden, but he was too weak even to think of riding the ten miles to London. Lady Penn was in tears as she drew her son aside and said,

"The doctor says that the fall of the first leaf will carry him away."

She gave William the rest of the family news. Margaret had just given birth to a baby girl. His young brother Richard was a little wild and traveling in Italy.

Margaret Penn looked up at this tall, strange son of

hers. Could he not give up his radical ideas and ways? she pleaded. His family needed him. He could fill his father's shoes and become a great man.

He shook his head. No, he could not give up being a Quaker. It was God's will.

Who would look after the Irish lands? she asked.

His steward, Philip Ford, had remained in Ireland to do that, he told her.

In London, Penn found that there was much more that he could do for Friends. Margaret Fell Fox was in prison; so was Gulielma's stepfather, Isaac Penington. He talked with George Fox and other Quaker leaders.

"The difficulty is that an old law, the Conventicle Act, has been renewed," they told him, "and persecutions have increased as a result."

Penn knew the law. It forbade meetings of any assembly, conventicle, or meeting, under pretense of religion, in any other manner than the Church of England. The law was really supposed to apply only to those meetings of persons plotting against the government.

"The Conventicle Act does not apply to Quaker meetings," George Fox explained.

Fox had already tested the law. He had preached to a group, and had been arrested and brought before the Lord Mayor of London. He had argued his case carefully and had convinced the court that the Conventicle Act did not apply to a Friends' meeting.

William Penn remembered his legal training at Lincoln's Inn. He knew that a legal precedent was the best argument in the world. He decided to be another test case.

On First Day Morning, as the Friends called Sunday, Willam Penn went to the biggest and most important Friends' Meeting in London. It was called Gracechurch Street Meeting, on the corner of Gracechurch and Lombard Streets. The authorities had boarded up the doors and windows, and soldiers stood on guard to prevent the Quakers from entering their building.

Penn was still a new convert, full of zeal. He smiled happily as he saw the group of Friends gathered in front of the building. They were making no effort to enter. With their usual gentle stubbornness they were simply holding their meeting in the street. He hastened to join them, and they stood together in silent worship.

In a very short while Penn felt moved to speak, and he began to preach to the group. That was what the authorities were waiting for. The Lord Mayor's men rushed in and seized Penn and one other, William Mead, and dragged them away.

"I see where they are taking us," he said to Mead, for the soldiers were leading them to the western end of London—to Newgate Prison. They were to be tossed into the same dungeon with debtors, murderers, and highwaymen, or so they thought. But William Penn was still the son of Sir William who was a close friend of the King. The Mayor's men didn't quite dare to throw him into the foul dungeon of Newgate Prison.

Instead, they detained him at a nearby inn, the Sign of the Black Dog.

Penn wrote to his father right away, begging him not to worry. The whole affair would amount to nothing, he explained. They were accused of rioting, which was entirely untrue. "I doubt not but I may be at liberty in a day or two, to see thee. I am very well, and have no trouble upon my spirits, besides my absence from thee . . . and what they have to charge me with is harmless." Feelings between father and son had healed a great deal.

But when Penn and Mead were brought into the Court of Quarter Sessions in the courthouse known as the Old Bailey, they soon realized that the situation was far from harmless. They had been arrested on Sunday, August 14, 1670, and their trial began the next day.

Penn saw at once that the court was prejudiced against him. He looked up at the men on the bench. There was the Lord Mayor, Sir Samuel Starling, the Recorder, five aldermen, and three sheriffs. They were positively jubilant over the fact that they had at last caught the son of Sir William Penn in the act of breaking a law. They had him, the rascal of a young radical! He had escaped from the Tower. He had not once been arrested in Ireland, while he worked to free others from prison. Well, he wouldn't get away this time. Penn looked at the twelve men in the jurybox. They were more sober about it.

The two defendants listened to the indictment: they

"with force and arms . . . in the street called Gracechurch Street, unlawfully and tumultuously did assemble and congregate themselves together, to the disturbance of the peace of the said Lord the King. And the aforesaid William Penn and William Mead . . . did preach and speak . . ."

"What say you William Penn and William Mead, are you guilty as you stand indicted?"

"We plead not guilty in manner and form."

That consumed the morning session, and they were required to wait all during the afternoon session while other prisoners were tried. Next morning, proceedings got under way in earnest. When Penn and Mead were brought before the Lord Mayor, the first device used against them was a trick that could always be played on Quakers—the hat service. In the scuffle of being arrested both men had lost their hats.

"Put on their hats!" ordered the Lord Mayor.

An officer placed strange hats upon their heads and led them forward to the bar.

"Do you know where you are?" the Recorder demanded.

Penn replied that he did, that he knew it to be a court, he supposed the King's court.

"Do you know there is respect due to the court?"

"Yes."

"Why do you not pay it then?"

"I do so."

"Why do you not put off your hat then?"

"Because I do not believe that to be any respect."

"Well, the court sets forty marks apiece upon your heads, as a fine, for your contempt of the court."

"I desire," said Penn, "it may be observed, that we came into the court with our hats off and if they have been put on since, it was by order from the bench; and therefore not we, but the bench, should be fined."

His remark was ignored and the trial got under way. Witnesses were called. One witness had seen Mr. Penn speaking to the group, but he had to admit he had not heard what Mr. Penn was saying. Two more said the same thing. The third witness couldn't remember whether he had seen Mead there or not.

"What say you, Mr. Mead," asked the Recorder, "were you there?"

"It is a maxim in your own law," Mead replied, "that no man is bound to accuse himself."

The case was becoming so flimsy that spectators in the courtroom began to be noisy and riotous.

"Silence in the court!"

Then Penn stated his case: "We confess ourselves to be so far from recanting, or declining to vindicate the assembling of ourselves, to preach, pray, or worship the eternal, holy, just God, that we declare to all the world, that we do believe it to be our indispensable duty, to meet incessantly upon so good an account; nor shall all the powers upon earth be able to divert us from reverencing and adoring our God, who made us."

"You are not here for worshiping God," put in one of the sheriffs, "but for breaking the law."

Penn promptly affirmed he had broken no law, and

desired to know by what law he was being prosecuted.

"Upon the common law."

"Where is the common law?"

The Recorder contemptuously ordered Penn to plead to the indictment.

Penn replied, "Shall I plead to an indictment that hath no foundation in law?"

"You are a saucy fellow; speak to the indictment."

"I say it is my place to speak to a matter of law; I am arraigned a prisoner; my liberty, which is next to life itself, is now concerned."

Penn argued as long as they would listen. That wasn't very long. Their patience gave out when Penn declared:

"I must plainly tell you, that if you will deny me the hearing of that law, which you suggest I have broken, you do at once deny me an acknowledged right, and evidence to the whole world your resolution to sacrifice the privileges of Englishmen to your sinister and arbitrary designs."

"Take him away!" shouted the Recorder.

"Take him away!" echoed the Mayor. "Take him away to the bale-dock."

Attendants rushed forward and dragged Penn to a corner of the room where they locked him into a tiny cupboard shaped like a cylinder.

After putting Mead through the same questions and after listening to Mead's arguments until their patience broke again, the Recorder decided to give the case to the jury.

Penn watched and listened from the bale-dock, until he heard the jury being told to bring in a verdict of guilty at their peril. At that he poked his nose between the bars of the bale-dock and shouted:

"I appeal to the jury, who are my judges, and this great assembly, whether the proceedings of the court are not most arbitrary, and void of all law, in offering to give the jury their charge in the absence of the prisoners . . ."

"Why ye *are* present," observed the Recorder sarcastically. "You *do* hear. Do you not?"

Penn's soul burst its bounds at that, and he forgot all his Quaker principles of gentleness and non-violence. In a rage he clambered to the top of the paling and shouted over it:

"No thanks to the court, that command me into the bale-dock; and you of the jury take notice, that I have not been heard. Neither can you legally depart the court, before I have been fully heard, having at least ten or twelve material points to offer, in order to disprove the charges."

"Pull that fellow down! Pull him down!" the Recorder commanded.

"Are these according to the rights of Englishmen?" shouted Mead.

Suddenly everyone was shouting, and to put an end to the confusion the prisoners were taken away and the jury was sent to the jury room.

The jury was out a long time. When the twelve finally filed back into the jury box they were asked:

"How say you? Is William Penn guilty of the matter, or not guilty?"

"Guilty of speaking in Gracechurch Street," said the foreman of the jury.

The mayor, aldermen and sheriffs were red in the face with anger. They wanted a verdict of guilty that they could punish. Penn had to be guilty of preaching to an unlawful and tumultuous assembly.

"You shall not be dismissed till we have a verdict that the court will accept!" declared the Recorder. "And you shall be locked up without meat, drink, or fire. We will have a verdict, or you shall starve for it."

William Penn stepped forward to defend the jury system:

"My jury ought not to be thus menaced. Their verdict should be free and not compelled. What hope is there of ever having justice done, when juries are threatened, and their verdicts rejected?"

Then Penn spoke to the jurymen: "You are Englishmen; mind your privilege. Give not away your right."

The jury was locked up all night. Still they refused to indict Penn and Mead. They declared they were acting according to their consciences.

"It is intolerable that my jury should be thus menaced," declared Penn.

"Stop his mouth," shouted the Mayor. "Bring fetters, and stake him to the ground."

"Do your pleasure," said Penn proudly. "I matter not your fetters."

The jury was locked up for another night. At last they did change their verdict somewhat—to a clear-cut "not guilty."

The court was beside itself. Penn and Mead demanded their liberty, since they had been cleared by the jury.

"Oh, no," said the Mayor. "You are in for your fines."

The fines were the result of the hat episode at the beginning of the trial. Once more Mead and Penn were led away to Newgate, because they would not pay the unjust fines.

The jurymen were punished for their "wrong" verdict. They were fined forty marks a piece. They listened and smiled at one another. Penn had told them, "Give not away your right." They, too, refused to pay their fines and were dragged off to prison.

In a few weeks eight of the jurymen were too worried about their businesses and their families, and they paid their fines and went free. But the other four decided to remain and be a test case no matter how long it took. They retained lawyers and appealed their case to a higher court, the Court of Common Pleas. Eventually a great and important decision was handed down: that a jury must always be allowed to render a free verdict, and that it may never be punished for its verdict.

William Penn and William Mead were detained only a few days after their trial ended. They planned to stick it out, and Penn wrote to his father, "I entreat thee not to purchase my liberty."

Sir William was very ill, and he needed William with him. He paid the fines for Penn and Mead so that his son could come home.

Penn hurried to Wanstead and found his father in bed, failing rapidly.

"I have written to the King," said Sir William, "and I have asked his protection for you. Both the King and the Duke of York sent personal messages promising me that they will look after you when I am gone."

He sank back on his pillow, and seemed to grow weaker almost at once. In another few days he was delirious. Only now and then could he talk to his wife and son.

Very shortly before Sir William died, he admitted how much he admired the Quakers.

"Son William, keep to your plain way of preaching, and keep to your plain way of living. . . . Shun all manner of evil. And I pray God to bless you all."

He died on September 16, 1670, and William Penn became the owner of his lands in England and Ireland and head of the family as well.

William Penn missed his father very deeply. They had been close all their lives, even with all their differences. To forget his grief, he left Wanstead for a while and went to Amersham to visit with the Peningtons and Gulielma Springett.

The authorities were still watching him, waiting for him to break another law. He did—that same winter. In February he attended a meeting in Wheeler Street in London. There were the usual soldiers already stationed at the door. Penn went past them and inside. No sooner had Penn arisen in place to speak to the meeting than the soldiers stomped forward and nabbed him. They took him straight to the Tower of London, and in another few hours he was standing once more before the Lord Mayor of London.

Surely they could not hope to convict him, he argued. Just the previous summer a jury had acquitted him and proved that the Conventicle Act did not apply.

The men on the bench winked at one another.

"You are not arrested under the Conventicle Act this time," they informed Penn, "but under the Five Mile Act."

The Five Mile Act forbade any non-conforming clergyman to preach within five miles of any city.

But *he* was not an ordained clergyman!

They paid no attention to his arguments. They had him this time, and they were not going to let him go. He was to serve six months in Newgate.

"Is that all?" Penn asked in surprise. "Thou well knowest a larger imprisonment has not daunted me!"

They knew that; they knew they hadn't accomplished anything. Penn would soon be out of prison and back preaching in meetings.

The court requested a corporal and a file of musketeers to accompany the prisoner.

"No, no," replied Penn. "Send thy lackey; I know the way to Newgate."

There were to be six months from the fifth of February, 1671, with no sight of family or Gulielma—six months of health-destroying foul air right into the heat of July.

Newgate was crowded with prisoners. Penn could have purchased private quarters, but he did not. He chose to dwell in the loathsome common quarters. There were plenty of Quakers already there to keep him company, mingled with every kind of felon. During the day the prisoners were permitted to walk in the hall which was on the second floor, and there were other rooms where they could move about and work. At night, though, they were all herded into one room—a huge, circular place, with a great oak pillar in the center. Prisoners strung their hammocks from the central pillar to the wall, in three tiers because there were so many of them. Those on the top tier had to climb up to bed first. The sick and dying lay on pallets scattered about the floor.

He passed the time writing tracts that he knew the Quakers needed. His most important Newgate tract was the one called *The Great Case of Liberty of Conscience*. He had really begun to write the tract in Ireland, but had had no time to finish it until now.

"By liberty of conscience," says the tract, "we understand not only a mere liberty of the mind, in believing or disbelieving this or that principle or doctrine, but the exercise of ourselves in a visible way of worship."

In another place it states, "It was the saying of a person once, too great to be named now, that liberty of conscience is every man's natural right, and he who is deprived of it, is a slave in the midst of the greatest liberty."

The wretched six months finally ended, and William Penn went free. He hurried straight to Gulielma Springett.

CHAPTER SIX

Gulielma

THE VIGOROUS AND HEARTY PENN recovered from his prison experience in a very short time. Soon he was attending meetings and working with Friends in Buckinghamshire and in London, often with Gulielma and the Peningtons and the Foxes.

George Fox was going to America. America? It was a wild, untamed world thousands of miles away. Quakers were persecuted in the New England part of America sometimes more cruelly than in England. The first

Quaker missionaries to go to America had been seized as witches when their ship reached Boston. Meetings flourished in America anyway, in Virginia, Maryland, eastern New Jersey, Long Island, and Rhode Island.

Quakers in England often talked of having a colony of their own in the New World. But as often as they talked of it, just so often did they shake their heads. No. It was impossible. Land grants in America were plums for royal favorites.

William Penn and Gulielma Springett and several others traveled down the Thames River from London in a barge to see George Fox off on his journey to America. They said farewell to him at Gravesend, then they turned back to London. They had much to talk over on the return trip, because they were planning to be married.

"Our marriage will be a blessed one," said Gulielma. "Thou art content to wait a while?"

She knew what troubled him. He felt called to go on a missionary journey of his own—through Holland and Germany.

"Thy duty to God must come first," she said quietly.

"I shall be gone but a few weeks."

"A few weeks are a very small part of a lifetime. How many lifetimes wilt thou create for others in those few weeks away from me!"

William Penn sailed across the English Channel to Holland the end of August. With him went Thomas Rudyard, a Quaker who had been in Newgate at the same time as he. The two men spent September and most of October in Holland and Germany, traveling from town to town, speaking to meetings, explaining the Quaker faith. An English Quaker merchant, Benjamin Furly, lived in Rotterdam. He acted as their translator when they spoke to Dutch groups.

Penn, Rudyard, and Furly visited a multitude of small villages and towns in Holland, and they stopped in the city of Amsterdam with her tree-lined canals and stately brick houses. At last, they crossed Dollart Bay to Emden in Germany.

Emden was so close to Holland that it looked Dutch with dikes, windmills, and canals. In Emden William Penn met Dr. and Mrs. Johann Haesbert. The Haesberts were deeply religious and their ideas were very like the Quakers. In a short time they adopted the Quaker faith and helped Penn start a meeting in their city.

"Farewell, Friend," they said to Penn when he left. "Thy message will flourish here."

The three travelers went on to Herford in Germany. They payed a call on a prominent and famous woman there, Princess Elizabeth of the Palatine, who had become Abbess of the Protestant Convent of Herford. The Abbess was a brilliant and scholarly woman, who already knew about the Quakers. She was partly Stuart; King Charles II of England was her first cousin. In later years she did a great deal to help the persecuted Quakers.

When Penn returned to Gulielma, she held both of his hands and smiled.

"Thou art weary."

"Weary, but happy," he told her. "Our journey did much good. We reached many new people and gave encouragement to those already working with small meetings against great odds."

"The oath troubles Friends here," she told him.

He nodded; he had heard. Friends refused to take oaths or to swear with one hand on the Bible. Truth is truth, they said. Swearing on the Bible does not improve a man's ability to tell the truth. In fact, they maintained, the Bible says to swear not at all.

The oath was one more way the authorities had of tripping up Quakers when they were arrested. "Will you take the oath?" the magistrate would ask. "No; I cannot," the prisoner would reply. "Then off to prison with you."

"More and more Quakers are being imprisoned because of the oath," said Gulielma.

And many were dying in prison from the crowded, dirty conditions.

"This cannot continue forever," Penn said, half out loud, half to himself. "There is a limit to how much suffering people can endure."

Gulielma shared his every concern. They talked for long hours together about the suffering Friends and how best to help them. Penn knew he had chosen a wife who would be courageous and helpful and devoted.

In spite of all their suffering, Friends were happy folk. When they felt God's presence in their meeting for worship, it gave them a deep sense of joy. When they traveled around the country gathering in new members, they were jubilant. And when a wedding occurred among them—then!—excitement really ran high.

So it was when Gulielma Springett and William Penn appeared before the monthly business meeting to declare their intent to wed. That was the custom of Friends. They held meetings for worship every First Day and business meetings once a month. William and Gulielma had to appear before two successive Monthly Meetings and receive the approval of the members. They had no difficulty in obtaining the approval, since Friends had been waiting eagerly for this wedding to happen. A wave of happiness spread through the meetings as preparations got under way.

William and Guli planned to live in the village of Rickmansworth, not far from Amersham. Their wedding took place on April 4,1672, in a house called King John's Farm in nearby Chorleywood. The Quakers gathered in the low-ceilinged living room, with its fireplace and heavy oak beams, its casement windows and floor of hand-hewn planks.

A Quaker wedding is solemn and beautiful, and the ceremony is like no other, since there isn't any minister or preacher. The bride and groom sit side by side in the meeting as its silence deepens into worship, and after a time, when they feel that members have had sufficient opportunity to dwell upon the sacred union, the couple stand up and clasp hands. In the simplest language they take one another for man and wife, promising to be loving and faithful as long as they both shall live. That is all. No ring, no flowers, no vows of obedience. They sit down again and the meeting continues its silent meditation. At last one member after another rises to give a message, that is, to say a few words of blessing and encouragement. After the meeting for worship is ended, the marriage contract is spread upon a table and the bride and groom sign their names. Then as many as wish sign as witnesses.

There were some fifty persons at King John's Farm for the wedding. William Penn's mother came from Wanstead, and so did his brother Richard. Isaac and Mary Penington and several of their children were there, as well as Thomas Rudyard. As soon as the serious part of the day was over, the solemnity vanished and happy conversation and laughter and congratulations began. The bride and groom wanted to escape, but they could not get away from the joyful throng for quite a while. They stood together in the middle of the room, glowing with happiness, while hosts of well-wishers shook their hands and kissed them.

At last they were out of the door and into their carriage, and driving away down Shepherd's Lane to the village of Rickmansworth. There in a big, many-gabled house, called Basing House, they settled down. They had both been living very unsettled and harassed lives until then, never knowing when they would be arrested or molested by the authorities. Here at last was a little peace and security.

For the first five years of their marriage they lived

fairly quietly and close to home. Rickmansworth was a short drive from London, and William and Guli continued to see their London friends. Philip Ford, who had returned from Ireland, still looked after Penn's financial affairs and properties. That left Penn's time entirely free for Quaker matters. He wrote tracts, preached at meetings, took part in public debates—anything George Fox thought necessary. George Fox was a great leader, and William Penn knew it. He would do anything for George Fox. During those first five years of his marriage he wrote at least twenty-five tracts, and some of them were as long as modern books. Since there were no newspapers to print the truth in those days, each tract that came out attacking the Quakers had to be answered with a truthful one. How people loved debating in the seventeenth century, either in print or on the debating platform! It was a form of free entertainment, and there was little to compete with it.

William and Gulielma had been married about a year when George Fox returned from America—full of news for the Quaker meetings! Friends, including the Penns, hurried from everywhere to hear Fox. Fox always glowed so with his message that his homespun eloquence electrified any meeting he talked to. He had landed in the West Indies, had visited Barbados and Jamaica, and then sailed to Virginia. He had traveled through bogs, rivers, creeks, and wild woods from Virginia to New England. Friends were increasing in the New World, Fox reported. They were already strong in Maryland and Rhode Island.

William and Guli held hands tightly as they listened to Fox. Friends increasing! Yet still suffering! Even where they had temporary peace they didn't know how long it would last.

The Penns returned to Rickmansworth, and George Fox began to travel about England, looking after his Children of the Light. But not for long. William Penn and others in and around London soon heard that George Fox had been arrested and clapped into Worcester Jail. Anxiously they held a meeting.

"We must do everything in our power to obtain George Fox's release," they agreed.

Quakers who were lawyers began to prepare his case for trial. Others felt that a personal appeal to the King should also be tried.

"William Penn, none has as much influence with the King as thou," they said.

"Six years have passed since I visited the royal court," said Penn.

That was how long he had been a Quaker. His appearance had changed a great deal. He no longer wore laces and velvets and plumes. His britches, stockings, and jacket were of the plainest. His once ornate wig was now a little civil thing, just enough to hide his baldness and keep his head warm. His face was more seasoned, and no longer boyish looking. He was nearly thirty.

"I think I shall call at the palace of the Duke of York first," he said to Guli. "In the past I have felt closer to him."

When William Penn and the King's brother James finally met, the meeting was momentous. It renewed the old, old friendship between the two families—the Penns and the Stuarts—that went back to both of their grandfathers. Penn and the Duke talked a long time about persecution.

"I am against all persecution for the sake of religion," the Duke told Penn. "I shall prevail upon the King to pardon Geoge Fox."

James was a Catholic, and in England the Catholics were also a persecuted minority.

The Duke kept his promise and the King did issue a pardon. The pardon helped, along with all the other efforts of Fox's lawyers, in obtaining Fox's release. But he was released only after fourteen months in a dark and dirty dungeon.

When Penn saw how badly Fox's health was affected by Worcester Prison, his concern for suffering minorities grew even deeper. When were Englishmen going to stop persecuting one another? When would they ever learn to respect one another's rights?

CHAPTER SEVEN

Penn's New Jersey Colony

AT HOME IN BASING HOUSE life was more hopeful. On January 25, 1675, Springett Penn was born. William's and Guli's son!

Actually, Springett was the fourth baby that Gulielma had had. The first, a girl named Gulielma for her mother, had died in a few weeks. The next year, Gulielma had had twin babies, a boy and a girl named William and Mary. The boy had died in about three months and the girl a little later. Babies did not always survive in the seventeenth century. There was simply not enough medical knowledge.

William and Gulielma watched Springett anxiously. They didn't want to lose this fourth child. But the boy grew bright and lively as the months passed.

William Penn wondered whether his son would grow up to be persecuted. It could certainly happen unless some solution was found in the meantime. Wherever he went in England he found non-conformists being mistreated. In county after county, in Leicestershire, Norfolk, Cambridgeshire, Oxfordshire, Cheshire and Yorkshire, Quakers were being impoverished by fines. Their properties were being destroyed. They were being imprisoned and mistreated. Whenever he sat in silent meditation, either with others or alone, he knew and felt in his heart that a way had to be found to ease such suffering—a way or a *place*. And he knew that it had to be found by the leaders, by such men as George Fox and himself.

He and Fox talked about America many times. But there was no free land there. Up and down the entire Atlantic Coast the land had all been parceled out.

Suddenly, as though in answer to their prayers, a piece of land in the New World dropped right into Penn's lap. It was the western part of New Jersey. In an instant, Penn was excited, on his feet, striding up and down. Of course! Of course!

England had captured a great piece of American land from the Dutch in 1664—in one of the wars with Holland in which Sir William Penn had been a naval hero.

The land was New Netherland. King Charles II then made the Duke of York its Proprietor. The Duke of York in turn bestowed a piece of New Netherland upon two royal pets, Sir George Carteret and John, Lord Berkeley. The piece consisted of New Jersey plus Staten Island. Berkeley and Carteret dreamed of great profits from the land rents (called quitrents) that settlers would pay. They sent out tracts and circulars persuading settlers to go to New Jersey. Many did go, and some moved in from other colonies. The towns of Bergen (now part of Jersey City), Monmouth, Elizabethtown, and Milford (now Newark) began to develop. Farms dotted the countryside near these settlements.

But Berkeley and Carteret were not good managers. They had difficulties with the government of the colony. At one point the settlers rose up in armed revolt against paying quitrents which they felt were unfair. Berkeley and Carteret never saw any big profits, and almost no colonists went to the western half of New Jersey. At last Berkeley decided to sell out his half, the western half, and he did—to a man named John Fenwick in trust for Edward Billinge. Fenwick and Billinge were both Quakers, but Berkeley was so disgusted with the whole situation that he didn't care who bought West New Jersey.

Fenwick and Billinge were worse managers. They were soon quarreling bitterly, chiefly over who owned how much of West New Jersey. It was the custom of Friends to settle their differences in the meeting, instead of going to a court of law. The meeting therefore asked William Penn to act as impartial arbitrator.

No wonder William Penn, who had been worrying so earnestly about finding a place for persecuted minorities, should jump up and pace the floor with happy excitement. Who could tell? Who could tell? Maybe this was it!

His legal experience came in handy right away, and so did his property experience in Ireland. First, Penn worked out a settlement that Fenwick and Billinge would agree to: one-tenth to Fenwick and nine-tenths to Billinge. But Billinge was in debt to so many people, who began to clamor for their money, that he appealed to the Friends' Meeting for further help. The Meeting appointed three trustees to manage Billinge's share, which was really most of West New Jersey. The trustees were William Penn, Gawen Lawrie, and Nicholas Lucas.

William Penn had been working out the New Jersey tangle at the same time that he was trying to get George Fox out of prison. He always had plenty of irons in the fire. He was made a trustee of West New Jersey at just about the time that Fox was set free. That meant that he and George Fox could plan the first Quaker colonial experiment together.

Fox was joyful over the idea of a Quaker colony in the New World. Here was an opportunity to apply their beliefs to a real life situation. Quakers believed in the equality of all men. They believed in the right of everyone to worship God in his own way. They believed in love and justice and honesty. Here was a chance to prove that their beliefs would work in daily life.

Many Quakers were eager to embark right away.

"No," said Penn. "We must clear up all the legal questions first so that there won't be any misunderstandings, and we must design a government."

He then sat down with a large group of prospective colonists to write the *Concessions and Agreements,* really a frame of government for West New Jersey. It proved to be a great and important document. "We have put the power in the people," it said in its preamble. The colonists were to choose their representatives in an assembly, and they were to choose their own governor. No one was to be arrested or imprisoned without just cause, and everyone was to have a trial by jury and freedom of worship. The Indians were to be treated fairly and equally. They were to be paid for their land. If an Indian broke a law, his jury must consist of six Indians and six colonists. One set of laws for everybody! When the *Concessions and Agreements* were completed, there were 151 signers.

William Penn did not intend to go to America with the New Jersey adventurers. He was the planner and designer. Plenty of capable people were going who could start the colony. Penn felt that he was needed by Quakers in Great Britain and Europe. The first ship to set sail under Penn's direction was the *Kent,* and aboard her were 230 adventurers, mostly Quakers.

A few weeks before the *Kent* sailed, William and Gulielma Penn moved from Basing House in Rickmansworth to southern England, to a big brick manor house on top of a hill in the parish of Worminghurst. Penn liked a quiet retreat in the country, and he liked being high on a hill with vast distances all around him. To the north of his Worminghurst house he could see a long sweep of green, forest-covered hills called the North Downs. To the south he could see more forest-covered hills, the South Downs. Just beyond the South Downs was the southern coast of England and the open sea. In fact, they were only fifteen miles from Brighton. The air at Worminghurst even smelled brackish when the wind was from the south.

Springett was two-and-a-half years old. His health seemed to grow stronger with each passing season, and the brisk sea air made his cheeks pink as apples.

"He seems more like thee every day," Penn told his wife.

And it was true. Springett was showing every sign of becoming gentle and kind and sensitive, just like his mother.

"I would rather have him lusty and impatient like thee," said Gulielma.

Quakers in southern England were overjoyed when the Penn family came to live among them. Penn was a fine minister, and he would give their meetings great strength. He would give them the courage they needed to face the persecutions that had been rather severe in these parts. There was no meeting house in the area yet, and so meetings were held in the big Worminghurst house every other First Day morning. On alternate First Days they met down in Thakeham Village at the home of John Shaw. On those Sundays, the Penns hitched a pair of oxen to a wagon and drove down the hill and through the woods to the Shaw house. They had to use oxen instead of horses, because the land in the valley was boggy.

Penn laid down a careful schedule for his family at home. They began each day by meeting for prayers, and they held a second prayer meeting before supper. Everyone rose in the spring and fall months at six in the morning, in the summer months at five, and in the dark English winter months at seven. Breakfast was about nine, dinner about twelve and supper about seven. Every servant after supper must come and render to his master and mistress an account of what had been done that day and receive instructions for the next. At the end of the day all gates and doors must be bolted, all fires and candles extinguished and all persons in bed by ten.

Gulielma did most of the managing of the household, while her husband had his Quaker activities. He soon began to feel a new concern.

"Another journey through Holland and Germany," he explained to Gulielma.

"If God calls thee, then thou must go," she said bravely.

"I have talked with George Fox, Robert Barclay, and others. Barclay was in Germany last year, and has told us much of sufferings there."

"Thou art not traveling alone!" Guli announced firmly.

"No. There will be a large party of Friends going.

Fox, Barclay, and George Keith will be among us."

He thought for a moment, and then he added, "I dislike leaving thee at this time."

Guli was expecting another child.

She laughed merrily. "There are the servants, and all our good neighbors. Thou wilt return in ample time."

Penn gave a long list of instructions to the servants about the care of the grounds: vegetable gardens, fruit trees, horses, oxen, cows; and of the house: meals, fireplaces, the many chambers. He would be severe with them, he promised, if he found things in disarray on his return.

He set out for London on the 22nd of July, 1677, and did not return until the end of October. On his way to Harwich to go aboard a packet boat, he stopped at Wanstead to visit his mother. She still lived in the big country house. She was overjoyed to see her son, to hear news of her grandson Springett, to discuss her financial affairs with him.

"If thou needest help in my absence," he advised her, "speak to Philip Ford."

At Harwich nine Quakers and two servants assembled for the missionary journey through Holland and Germany, and the most important of them were Fox, Penn, Barclay, and Keith. They made Rotterdam their first stop, because they wanted to see Benjamin Furly. Furly had been working hard to translate Penn's tracts and writings into Dutch. Then the party divided up to cover as much territory as possible. Penn, Keith, Barclay, and Furly went on in open wagons across Holland and Germany. They wanted to visit the Princess Elizabeth in Herford again.

They spent three busy days in Herford, holding meetings with the townspeople and with Elizabeth and her staff. The Abbess of Herford became a true friend of the Quakers although she herself never joined.

Barclay returned to Holland, and Penn, Keith, and Furly pushed on. They traveled from town to town in Germany, through good weather and bad, sometimes in the pouring rain, but they never hesitated. They preached to any groups who were willing to listen. They handed out books on Quakerism in Dutch and German. Through Paderborn, Cassel, and Frankfurt. Some towns were hostile; in others Quaker meetings sprang up as a result of their visit. Small meetings that were already there grew larger. When they reached the Rhine River they turned northward and floated in boats down the Rhine toward Holland. To Mainz, where the Rhine Valley is wide and flat with rolling hills in the distance. To Coblenz, where the sides of the river are steep and mountainous and covered with dense forests with here and there an ancient castle. To Cologne and then to Duisburg, where the Ruhr River flows into the Rhine, and the valley is once more wide and flat and fertile.

In the town of Mülheim on the Ruhr the ruling prince was so annoyed at the thought of Quakers that he ordered them to move on.

"We have no need of Quakers here! Get you out of

my dominion. You shall not go to my town." And he detailed some soldiers to escort them beyond the limits of Mülheim.

At Duisburg the travelers were warned to be extremely cautious of the ruling prince. "For at some he sets his dogs, upon others he puts his soldiers to beat them."

William Penn was accumulating a deep feeling of concern as he went from town to town. Each time he saw an intolerant attitude or discovered groups being persecuted for their beliefs, he grew more tense.

When they reached Amsterdam once more, they met the rest of the Quaker travelers and compared notes.

William Penn tarried only a day with George Fox and the others. He had something else to do, and he was eager to be on his way. He set out with a Dutch Quaker, named Jan Claus, as his interpreter, and took a boat up a long canal to Leeuwarden. He paused long enough to visit a few meetings and then went on overland to the port of Delfzijl. Next morning he was in a boat crossing the bay to Emden.

Six years had passed since his last visit to Emden when he had met Dr. and Mrs. Haesbert. How had they made out? How big would the Quaker meeting be by now?

What he found was heartbreaking. He could only listen grief-stricken and silent as residents told him what had taken place. Twelve families had joined the Quaker meeting, and they had been barbarously used.

The meeting was now completely scattered and broken. The members had suffered fines and imprisonment. Many were expelled from the country altogether. Dr. Haesbert had been arrested again and again and finally died in prison. His wife was dead, too.

Penn went to his lodgings and sank into a chair, holding his head in his hands. Something *had* to be done. He took up a quill and tried to write a letter to the President of the Council of State. He didn't have the language to express what he felt. He threw down the quill.

"I must go myself to plead the innocent and suffering cause of our Friends with him," he told Claus.

The President of the Council was completely astonished by such a visit. He was so deeply impressed by Penn's earnestness and sincerity that he said,

"Compose a letter to the Senate and I will deliver it to them personally."

The result was no less astonishing! Persecutions in Emden stopped and Friends were permitted to meet in peace.

William Penn returned to Holland. There were more towns and villages to be visited and a final rendezvous in Amsterdam of all the Quaker travelers. Their fame had spread far and wide. The meetings held in Amsterdam were huge. They went on to The Hague and to Rotterdam, and at last the mission was completed.

When Penn arrived back in Worminghurst, Gulielma could see that he was deeply troubled.

"A way must be found," he told her. "A way must be found."

"There is news for thee," she said, and she smiled. "It is from America."

The *Kent* had reached New Jersey while he was in Germany. In August, 1677, she had made her way up the Delaware River and dropped anchor near the present site of Burlington. The Quaker adventurers had found the land really wild, but they had brought building bricks for ship's ballast, and their homes were already in the making. Most of them were experienced farmers, weavers, tailors, or shoemakers, and all of them were hard workers. They were bargaining with the Indians for the land, laying out the town of Burlington, and soon there would be meeting houses and schools. The soil was rich, the climate invigorating.

Penn wanted more news—more progress—more information about how the frame of government was working. Was this all? Was it all? Could he write to Friends in the Rhine Valley about a new haven in America?

"Patience, my dear," counseled Gulielma.

During the next weeks and months more news came from West New Jersey.

"The forests abound in venison, fowl, wild strawberries, and cranberries. The rivers are full of fish. The Indians are friendly and peaceful. They have taught us many new kinds of food, and a kind of corn is one of them. We are organizing our government, and we can see that our social experiment is going to be successful."

In the early spring the Penn's next child was born, a girl, named Letitia.

Spring also meant that the colonists had weathered their first winter successfully. The weather was colder than they were accustomed to, but their houses were rapidly going up.

The soil was indeed rich, and it soon began to produce more than they could use. They cleared forest and planted, cleared forest and planted. Experienced farmers that they were, they could see that in a few seasons they would have enough crops from their fruit orchards and grainfields to export all over America and even to Europe.

The West New Jersey colony prospered and lived at peace with its neighbors. More shiploads of adventurers continued to arrive. The settlers nodded happily when they saw their children playing with the Indian children, and when the Indian children came to the Friends' schools. News of the prosperous community in the New World traveled in epistles to the Old.

CHAPTER EIGHT

The Other Side of the Delaware

For three years after his return from the Continent, William Penn worked constantly on Friends' affairs in England. Persecution of non-conformist groups grew worse. At one time there was a wave of anti-Catholic hysteria, and great numbers of Catholics were unjustly arrested and mistreated. Many even lost their heads on the block. If it could happen to one group it could happen to another. Toleration must be for everyone to be successful. William Penn made two speeches before a special committee of the House of Commons about the true meaning of freedom of conscience as the Quakers saw it.

"For we must give the liberty we ask, and cannot be false to our principles, though it were to relieve ourselves, for we have good will to all men, and would have none suffer for a truly sober and conscientious dissent on any hand."

When the King called a national election to choose members to Parliament, it was a deeply bitter affair, full of tense rivalries and unfair practices. The Whig Party opposed the King and his Royalist Party. Parliament was growing stronger every day, and the King was competing with the Parliament for power. If too many Whigs were elected to the Parliament, the King would be less powerful.

The Whig Party had really developed out of the Puritan movement. It stood for religious toleration, and a strong Parliament elected by the people. Whigs were the liberals of their day. Most Quakers voted Whig.

Through it all, William Penn was friendly with the King and the Duke of York, even though he himself held Whig ideas. Time and again he went to the King to give him sound advice. "Persecution only strengthens the opposition," he warned the King. "If thou wert more tolerant, they would not try to limit thy powers." His advice did no good.

Penn was worried about England. What would eventually happen to England, if her best citizens had to flee? How could a nation be successful if such things as treachery and persecution of the just went on?

News continued to come from the West New Jersey colony. "Our orchards are bursting with peaches, apples, cherries, and our fields are rich with crops. From Burlington our trading ships take our produce down the Delaware to other American ports. We are a prospering and happy community."

Why was West New Jersey so much happier than England? The formula was simple: love—work—honesty.

The more trouble that Penn saw in England, the more worried he became. America *was* the solution, but the West New Jersey colony, stretching along the eastern shore of the Delaware River, wasn't big enough to hold everyone who wanted to go. Something *had* to be done. *He* had to do something.

But wait! The land on the western side of the Delaware River possessed the same rich soil, the same abundance, and it had scarcely any settlers. From the Delaware River it extended westward into raw, dense wilderness, known to none but the Indians. It, too, was part of the New Netherland grant belonging to the Duke of York.

No; it couldn't be. Penn was a Whig. The King could not give a land grant to a member of the opposition party. He could not risk his throne even for so close a personal friend.

Then Penn remembered something. There was an old, old debt that the King owed Sir William. It was for money borrowed from and wages owed to Penn's father as a naval officer, a sum of around sixteen thousand pounds.

Sir William would never have asked his King to repay a loan, but William Penn did. It was the only basis on which he could ask for land in America.

William Penn sent a formal petition to the King, asking for the piece of land lying west of the Delaware and north of Maryland, as repayment for the old debt owed his father.

It became clear at once that the King wanted to help Penn. Charles II received the petition the end of May, 1680, and the same day one of the secretaries of State presented it to the Privy Council. The members of the Council winked at one another. If Penn the Quaker founded a colony in America, whole shiploads of the opposition party would leave England. The gentlemen of the Council did their best to speed matters up. Everyone seemed pleased with the idea. The Duke of York readily gave his consent to letting Penn have another piece of New Netherland.

There was a little trouble with Lord Baltimore's representatives over the exact boundary line between Maryland and the Penn grant. Nobody in England had an accurate map or survey of the country. They thought the location of the fortieth degree of northern latitude would be all right for a boundary between the new colony and Maryland, even though they weren't exactly sure where the fortieth degree was. Penn said he thought that the boundary would fall about twelve miles north of the town of New Castle, on the west bank of the Delaware River.

At last Penn's grant was defined: it was to be "bounded on the east by Delaware River, from twelve miles distant northwards of New Castle town, unto the three and fortieth degree of northern latitude . . . to extend westward five degrees in longitude . . . and on the south, by a circle, drawn at twelve miles distance from New Castle, northward and westward, until the beginning of the fortieth degree of northern latitude; and then by a straight line westward . . ."

William Penn hurried to the Quakers in London with the wonderful news, even before his royal Charter was ready. He began at once with plans—vast plans! What a marvelous opportunity! Plenty of space for as many adventurers as wanted to go! The experimental community had worked in New Jersey. It would work on a vaster scale on the other side of the river. There would be no rank, no ruling family, no titled nobility. All men would be equal. Every man would have a voice in the government. There was so much to be done! A government must be designed, towns and townships laid out, farm tracts and town lots distributed.

The royal Charter, dated March 4, 1681, made William Penn absolute proprietor. He had to answer for his actions only to the King of England. Penn had power to rule as he wished. He could make laws. He could appoint the men who were to rule the colony. But William Penn had no intention of using such vast personal power. He planned to sign it away and to place the power in the people as he had done in West New Jersey. It would be more successful than before.

"For the matters of liberty and privilege, I purpose that which is extraordinary and to leave myself and successors no power of doing mischief, that the will of one man may not hinder the good of an whole country." So he wrote to the Friends.

Penn went to work with boundless energy and ardent faith. He needed brave adventurers, men with strong backs and wide vision, "men of universal spirits, that have an eye to the good of posterity," men with practical talents—husbandmen, craftsmen; and he needed anyone who needed hope.

He wrote to key men in major cities and appointed them as his agents. In Ireland he chose Robert Turner, a Quaker living in Dublin, whom he had met when he was there. In London Philip Ford became as important to him as his own right arm, with all the bookkeeping and paper work that had to be done. Thomas Rudyard was another in London. James Harrison, a shopkeeper in Bolton, was another. On the Continent it was Benjamin Furly. In Scotland it was Robert Barclay.

Penn wrote a long letter to Robert Turner in Dublin:

DEAR FRIEND:

My true love in the Lord salutes thee and dear Friends that love the Lord's precious Truth in those parts. Thine I have, and for my business here, know that after many waitings, watchings, solicitings and disputes in council, this day my country was confirmed to me under the Great Seal of England, with large powers and privileges, by the name of *Pennsylvania;* a name the King would give it in honor of my father. I chose New Wales, being, as this, a pretty hilly country, but Penn being Welsh for a head, as Penmanmoire in Wales, and Penrith in Cumberland, and Penn in Buckinghamshire, the highest land in England, called this Pennsylvania, which is the high or head woodlands; for I proposed, when the Secretary, a Welshman, refused to have it called New Wales, Sylvania, and they added Penn to it; and though I much opposed it, and went to the King to have it struck out and altered, he said it was past, and would take it upon him. . . . Thou mayest communicate my grant to Friends, and expect shortly my proposals.

It is a clear and just thing, and my God that has given it me through many difficulties, will, I believe, bless and make it the seed of a nation. I shall have a tender care to the government, that it be well laid at first. No more now, but dear love in the Truth.

Thy true friend,

WM. PENN

CHAPTER NINE

The Government of Pennsylvania

PENN'S ENTHUSIASM WAS TREMENDOUS, and it was contagious. Whenever he entered a Friends' meeting, the whole room tingled. After meeting, Friends swarmed around him happily for news of their great American adventure. Whenever he strode into the house at Worminghurst, there was a flurry of excitement and children running to greet him. By now he had three children. The third, William Penn, Jr., had been born March 14, 1680, about two months before

William Penn applied to the King for his Pennsylvania land grant.

The fortunes of Penn's entire family were involved in the Pennsylvania project. William and Gulielma, the five-year-old Springett, two-year-old Letitia, and the infant William, would all share its destiny.

"Some day we will all live in America," Penn promised them.

He would set sail first, to prepare a place for them to live, and they would follow later—family, servants, furniture.

Then off he hurried—to conferences with his agents, or to the mountain of correspondence on his writing table. He appointed William Markham, his first cousin, to be Deputy Governor. Markham was to go to America ahead of Penn, to set up a temporary government and make friends with the Indians. Penn and the Quakers were determined that there should be no occasion for wars in Pennsylvania. If they dealt honorably with the Indians, the Indians would have no cause to go on the warpath.

Penn sent out tracts describing the "Province of Pennsylvania in America," and explaining the terms under which land could be obtained. An adventurer could purchase or rent a piece of land in Pennsylvania. If he purchased, he had to buy at least 250 acres. A complete share consisted of five thousand acres and was called a propriety. The price was one hundred pounds plus fifty shillings quitrent (1 shilling for each 100 acres per year forever). He would receive a few town lots and the rest out in the country.

There was no private property as we know it today. The idea was just beginning to develop. The quitrent, which no longer exists, was an ancient feudal custom, handed down from the times when the King owned everything and all his subjects were tenants. In the days of knighthood, a knight paid his quitrent in gallant services to the king. A purchaser of land in Penn's day never quite owned his land completely. He had to keep paying his quitrent to keep his land.

An adventurer who wished only to rent land in Pennsylvania could have no more than 200 acres at a penny an acre per year.

The passage money aboard ship was six pounds per person (only five pounds for a servant) and fifty shillings for each child under ten. There was an extra charge for freight since the adventurers were taking all their household goods with them.

The frame of government was the thing nearest and dearest to Penn's heart. That would be the real test of everyone's hopes, the real test of Pennsylvania, the real test of Quakerism itself. He did not write it alone. Designing the government of a new country was too important a task to trust to the judgment of any one man. He consulted at least nineteen learned men in England and on the Continent. They all contributed their ideas.

The final *Frame of Government* contained a Preface and twenty-four Sections. "Any government is free to the people under it," said the Preface, "where the laws rule, and the people are a party to those laws." Then came a description of the government. There was to be a Council and General Assembly, an upper and lower house, to make the laws and handle public affairs. There was to be an automatic election every year to choose the members of the Council and Assembly. All freemen in the province would be entitled to vote. Anyone who lived in Pennsylvania and owned at least a hundred acres of land, or who paid "scot and lot" (tax) to the government, was a freeman. Anyone could become a freeman, even if he had once been a bond servant. Penn, the Governor, would preside over the Council. He and the Council would be the executive branch. They would enforce the laws, erect courts, plan towns, found schools, build ports, roads, and market places, and look after the treasury.

The New Jersey *Concessions* had of course furnished some of the ideas for the Pennsylvania *Frame,* even though Penn and his associates wrote a whole new document. For a second time Penn was putting the power in the people with elections and a representative government. Only, this time, he *knew* it would work. Many new ideas were used, and one of these was the amendment clause. The Pennsylvania *Frame of Government* could be amended by a vote of six-sevenths of the Council and Assembly with the consent of the Governor. This meant that the Pennsylvania *Frame* could grow and change with the changing times.

Along with the *Frame of Government* went forty laws which would eventually have to be approved by the Pennsylvania Assembly. They guaranteed freedom of speech and worship, and trial by jury. They abolished the death penalty on everything but treason and murder. The Quakers would have liked to abolish the death penalty altogether, but the royal Charter wouldn't allow them to. And there were laws against stealing, piracy, arson, swearing, lying, cockfights, and the like.

William Penn did not invent the ideas that he put into his *Frame of Government*. He used the most advanced thinking of his times. He took the new theories of government in which he and the Quakers believed and put them to the test. For instance, there were many who were beginning to doubt the divine right of kings. But the divine right of kings was still the law of the land in England, and so it was considered radical to be against it. In Pennsylvania there was to be no king.

There was to be human dignity in Pennsylvania—for everyone. *Liberty of conscience* was the key. A man could say what he thought in Pennsylvania and not be arrested for it. Every man's right over his own estate was to be respected. The whole people was to participate in making and enforcing the laws and in judging lawbreakers.

Pennsylvania was to be the seed of a great nation. Penn called it "an holy experiment."

CHAPTER TEN

Penn's Sailing

MEANWHILE, WILLIAM MARKHAM, Deputy Governor, was already in America. He had reached New York in June, 1681. Soon he began to send Penn encouraging reports. The handful of Europeans already living in Pennsylvania was ready to accept their new Governor and Proprietor.

William Penn felt deeply happy that people were willing to trust him—on both sides of the ocean. The Quakers trusted him completely. "I do judge William

Penn as fit a man as any in Europe to plant a country," one wrote to another. They trusted him so much that the first shipload of adventurers set sail long before the *Frame of Government* was completed.

In September, 1681, six months after the royal Charter, the first ship bound for Pennsylvania sailed out of Bristol, England. We think it was the *Bristol Factor*. Penn journeyed to Bristol to see her off. The next month he saw the *John and Sarah* sail from London.

What great hope went with those first adventurers! Soon he would follow them! Soon he would *know* just what the American wilderness was like!

Ships that came and went always carried a heavy packet of mail from Penn to Markham. He sent many letters of instruction to Markham and to his land commissioners. One of the items in the packet aboard the *John and Sarah* was Penn's famous letter to the Indians.

Penn gave a great deal of thought to the original inhabitants of the Delaware Valley. Quakers living on the eastern shore of the Delaware River said the Indians were friendly. Penn wanted that friendliness to continue, and so he wrote to the Indians of Pennsylvania:

MY FRIENDS:

There is one great God and power that hath made the world and all things therein, to whom you and I and all people owe their being and well-being, and to whom you and I must one day give an account, for all that we do in the world; this great God hath written

His law in our hearts, by which we are taught and commanded to love and help, and do good to one another, and not to do harm and mischief one unto another. Now this great God hath been pleased to make me concerned in your parts of the world, and the King of the country where I live hath given unto me a great province therein; but I desire to enjoy it with your love and consent, that we may always live together as neighbors and friends. . . . I have great love and regard towards you, and I desire to win and gain your love and friendship by a kind, just and peaceable life, and the people I send are of the same mind, and shall in all things behave themselves accordingly; and if in any thing any shall offend you or your people, you shall have a full and speedy satisfaction for the same, by an equal number of just men on both sides, that by no means you may have just occasion of being offended against them. I shall shortly come to you myself. . . . In the meantime, I have sent my commissioners to treat with you about land, and a firm league of peace; let me desire you to be kind to them and the people, and receive these presents and tokens which I have sent to you, as a testimony of my good will to you, and my resolution to live justly, peaceably and friendly with you.

I am your loving friend,
WILLIAM PENN

Planning to leave England was not easy for any of the adventurers. They had to close down their businesses, sell their houses, decide what to do with the furniture they could not take aboard ship. Hardest of all, they had to say good-by forever to friends and relations and native land.

It was just as difficult for the Penn family as for anyone else. William Penn had many personal affairs to finish up as well as all the details for Pennsylvania. His mother had died early in 1682, and he had to see that all her affairs were settled. He worked feverishly to get things done.

"The great difficulty is, my dear," he said to his wife, "that I am needed on both sides of the ocean at once."

Gulielma was expecting another child, and her mother, Mary Springett Penington, came down to Worminghurst to stay with her. Guli's stepfather, Isaac Penington, had died.

Late at night, when all his family were asleep, William Penn sat at his writing table. How could he leave them? He and Gulielma had been married for ten years; this was to be their first serious separation. And the children! The gentle Springett was seven; the lusty Letitia was four; and sturdy William, Jr., was two.

And if he should be lost at sea? Ships that set out did not always arrive. He could not begin to tell his family how much he was going to miss them, but he must at least leave some instructions. He picked up his quill and began to write.

MY DEAR WIFE AND CHILDREN:

My love, that neither sea, nor land, nor death itself, can extinguish or lessen toward you, most endearedly visits you with eternal embraces, and will abide with you forever; and may the God of my life watch over you and bless you, and do you good in this world and forever. Some things are upon my spirit to leave with you in your respective capacities, as I am to one a husband, and to the rest a father, if I should never see you more in this world.

My dear wife! remember thou wast the love of my youth, and much the joy of my life; the most beloved, as well as the most worthy of all my earthly comforts . . .

He wanted them never to forget the meeting for worship. He wanted his wife to keep careful household accounts and to give the children a good education. He thought of his three children. They were young enough to forget their father, and he didn't want that to happen. To each of them he wrote a separate letter.

My dear Springett:

Be good, learn to fear God, avoid evil, love thy book, be kind to thy brother and sister and God will bless thee and I will exceedingly love thee. Farewell dear child

Thy dear father,
Wm. Penn

Dear Letitia:

I dearly love thee and would have thee sober; learn thy book, and love thy brothers. I will send thee a pretty book to learn in. The Lord bless thee and make a good woman of thee. Farewell

Thy dear father,
WM. PENN

DEAR BILLE:

I love thee much, therefore be sober and quiet, and learn his book. I will send him one, so the Lord bless thee. Amen.

Thy dear father,
WM. PENN

And the Quaker meetings? He must leave them one last sermon. In the final few weeks before sailing, he wrote his tract, *No Cross, No Crown.* Thirteen years earlier, when he was in the Tower of London, he had written a short piece with the same title. The first one had been rather amateurish. The second is the finest thing he ever wrote, and it explains the Quaker faith.

A year had passed since the sailing of the *Bristol Factor* and the *John and Sarah.* At last it began to seem that William Penn would really be able to get away himself. He placed all of his financial affairs in England in Philip Ford's care. Ford had been his trusted steward for thirteen years.

"Thou art to receive all money due me while I am absent in America," he instructed Ford, "and out of those funds you are to pay my just debts. Thou wilt receive purchase money on my American lands as well, and rentals from my Irish estates."

Ford agreed. He was a very skillful bookkeeper and manager of money matters.

"Is thy annual salary of forty pounds adequate?"

Ford said that it was.

The Worminghurst house was in a turmoil of packing. Many of Penn's things were already aboard the ship at Deal.

"I shall come up to London with thee," said Gulielma. She was quiet and gentle, but she was also firm. He knew by the way she said it that he would have to let her come with him.

There was more turmoil around the Quaker meetings in London, they found. At least a hundred Friends were going to America on the same ship as Penn. Most of them were English, but there was at least one Irish family and one Welsh.

Before setting out for Deal from London, William Penn called at the home of Philip Ford and his wife Bridget. They had some bills and accounts that needed his signature to approve them. One statement seemed rather large to Penn, nearly three thousand pounds.

"That is for money we have laid out for thee," they told him. "Thou instructed us to purchase a great many things for thy voyage."

Penn never had enough patience to study out small details, and this day he was so beside himself with excitement at going to America, that he couldn't concentrate on the figures. Anyway, there wasn't time. He had to hurry on to Deal to get aboard his ship. He just snatched up the quill and with a flourish signed the paper and tossed it back to Ford. He didn't even think to ask Ford for a copy.

He dashed back to London, and he and Gulielma started out for the port of Deal. The Fords had come along, too.

Gulielma did not go all the way to Deal.

"I must take my final leave of thee."

After one last embrace they parted, and she returned to Worminghurst.

The Fords stuck to Penn all the way to Deal.

There was a terrific hubbub on the dock. Passengers going aboard with their things, and a great crowd of friends and relatives seeing them off. Children were running about and getting lost. There was shouting and crying and laughing.

In the midst of all that confusion, just before he went aboard, the Fords handed Penn three more papers to sign. "Just some accounts for thy approval," they said. Once again, in the rush and commotion, Penn signed.

Then William Penn joined the other adventurers aboard the *Welcome*. The *Welcome* was a ship of three hundred tons, 108 feet long, with three square-rigged masts. She was much larger and safer than the *Mayflower* had been.

The *Welcome* weighed anchor and spread her sails either on the last day of August or the first of September, 1682. As William Penn stood at the rail, watching the land gradually disappear from sight, he never expected to see England again.

CHAPTER ELEVEN

What Penn Found in America

THE *Welcome* NEEDED almost two months to cross the Atlantic Ocean. Two months of good weather and bad, smooth seas and rough. The passengers were crowded; there was very little water for washing; almost everyone had a spell of seasickness at some time or other. To make matters worse, an epidemic of smallpox broke out among them. Since William Penn had had smallpox as a child, he was immune, and he could help nurse the sick. Even with everything that everyone could do, all but thirty-one died. And in the midst of the difficulties, one new baby was born.

"Land ahoy!" the cry went up at last, and the bedraggled and weary travelers hurried to the rail. They caught their first glimpse of the forest-covered land, the wild and untamed land, where, they'd heard, the natives sometimes tomahawked and scalped those who tried to settle there.

The *Welcome* drew closer and turned slowly into Delaware Bay and began to make her way up the river. It was the end of October, and in the forests that covered the land on both sides of the river the leaves had begun to turn to brilliant colors—red, gold, rust. Penn gazed at the grandeur of the scene.

In a glowing sunset, the *Welcome* furled her sails and dropped anchor before the town of New Castle, the port that guarded the entrance to the upper Delaware. New Castle had been settled by the Dutch, and so it looked Dutch, with dikes holding the water back from the meadows and a windmill standing primly.

The shore was crowded with settlers and coppery-skinned, almost naked Indians, all curious about the arrival of the ship.

How eagerly the sea-weary travelers hurried into boats to be rowed ashore! William Markham stood with a group of officials to greet William Penn, the new Proprietor.

As William Penn stepped ashore he was almost overcome with emotion.

"In no outward thing have I known greater exercise,"

he said later. "I am firm in my faith that the Lord will prosper it."

With much formality he was escorted to the town's fort and there the town officials "surrendered" to the new Proprietor and Governor. And with more bowing and speech-making, William Penn was presented with a piece of turf with a twig planted in it and water and soil of the River Delaware.

William Penn, William Markham, and the rest of the adventurers returned to the *Welcome* and sailed on up the Delaware to the village of Upland. Upland was really just a small clearing in the woods with a few cabins, and there Robert Wade had a house and a boat landing. Markham had made it his headquarters, and so did Penn for the time being.

News of Penn's arrival had flown up the river ahead of him, and he found another huge crowd waiting to greet him. As the *Welcome* dropped anchor, canoes shot out into the water all around her.

Penn's upbringing as a courtier gave him great dignity. He walked erect with his head high, as a Governor and Proprietor should; and the Indians admired him for it. He in turn admired the Indians for their proud carriage.

Everyone marveled at Penn's energy. No sooner were the welcomings over, than he plunged into the work. His faith and enthusiasm and great executive ability began to show results at once.

"We will change the name of Upland to Chester," he announced, "and it will be our temporary capital.

Now I wish to talk to my land commissioners about the site of the permanent capital."

He had sent three land commissioners to America, and one of them was Thomas Holme, his Surveyor General. One of their tasks was to select a site for the new city he was going to found.

"Be sure to make your choice where it is most navigable, high, dry, and healthy," he had instructed them.

One of the first things he did was to travel on up the river to inspect the site Thomas Holme and the other commissioners had chosen. When he reached the place he was delighted. The banks of the Delaware rose in high bluffs there, and below the bluffs Dock Creek formed a natural pond just before it flowed into the Delaware—an excellent haven for sloops and schooners. The old Dutch West India Company had already found the spot, and they had put up a trading post there. Penn found ten houses standing in a row extending north from Dock Creek Pond. Some were brick and some were wood. The biggest was the Blue Anchor Tavern. It was brick, and it served as a post office, ferry house, exchange, and inn for trappers and fur traders.

William Penn and Thomas Holme sat down at one of the inn tables.

"The city is to be called Philadelphia," said Penn. "I have coined the name from two Greek words: *philos* meaning love and *adelphos* meaning brother."

Holme had drawn a plan of the streets of Philadelphia, and he spread his map on the table for Penn to inspect. Penn soon nodded and smiled—Holme knew what he wanted as Penn had given him clear instructions.

Penn remembered the crowded, dirty, and unhealthy streets of London and Paris. He remembered how the epidemic of plague had spread in London and how fire had gutted the city. His new city was to have no epidemics or fires. It was to have wide, straight streets running parallel. A wide avenue called High Street (now Market) was to run the length of the city through its center from the Delaware River to the Schuylkill River. Another thoroughfare called Broad Street would cross High Street. Each house was to have gardens and trees around it, because, Penn said, he wanted "a green country town which will never be burned and always be wholesome."

"I am pleased with thy plans," he said to Holme, "very pleased."

"Some of the settlers have already held a drawing for lots in the new town," the land commissioners reported.

"Fine!" said Penn. "Then let them proceed with the building."

In a few days he went on up the river another twenty-five miles with William Markham, to see Pennsbury Manor, the place where Penn was going to build a home for Gulielma and himself and the children.

"I am sure I have chosen a place to suit thy taste and temperament," said Markham.

Penn was overjoyed with Pennsbury Manor. It was a vast tract and lay along the Delaware for several miles northward from Neshaminy Creek. He planned to build a beautiful home there.

"The Indians were most friendly when I purchased this piece of land from them," said Markham.

Penn had had the Indians on his mind from the moment of his arrival, and long before that. His next task, and one of the most important was to hold a big conference with the neighboring tribes. The plans were made; the day was set. "I shall shortly come to you myself," he had promised in his famous letter to them, and he had kept that promise. And so word had gone out far and wide that the Chief Sachem of the settlers wished to meet in a peace conference with the Sachems of the Indian tribes. Penn had learned diplomacy at the royal Courts in England and France. He knew how to honor the kings of other lands.

We no longer know the exact date of the conference, and we no longer have absolute proof that it took place. But there is enough evidence to believe that it did. The Great Treaty must have made a magnificent scene under the tall old trees at Shackamaxon. The Indians came in their finest dress and beadwork, walking with great dignity. The Quakers were in their plain dress, and William Penn wore a blue sash to show that he was the highest ranking chieftain of his people.

The Indians who attended were mostly from the Delaware Valley. They were the Lenni Lenape—tall and broad-shouldered, narrow-waisted, regal in their manner. They went almost naked in summer except for moccasins and a breechclout. They added leggings and a blanket or animal skin around the body and across one shoulder in the winter. Their weather-browned skin was carefully greased with bear's fat as a protection against insects. The heads of the young men were shaved all except the coarse black hair of a tuft on the top, left as a challenge to their enemies. Their art was beadwork; their money was wampum made of shells; their weapons were the tomahawk and bow and arrow. They rode unshod horses and used canoes made by hollowing out the trunk of a tree with fire and a sharp stone. They earned their living chiefly by hunting and fishing. They lived in wigwams fashioned like an inverted bowl of woven sapling poles covered with bark.

The Lenape already knew the Quakers as a result of the West New Jersey settlement, and so at the Great Treaty they were ready and willing to trust Penn's promises of peace and honor.

The Sachems talked a long time. They agreed to live together in love and harmony and to respect one another's rights.

Soon after that Penn began to study the Lenape language so that he could converse with them without an interpreter. He visited in their homes and ate their food in their way. He joined in their games and sports, and they admired his athletic strength. Even though he was thirty-eight, he out-jumped and out-ran warriors younger than himself. The Lenape took him to their hearts, and the day soon came in Pennsylvania when an Indian could pay a white man no higher compliment than to tell him he was like William Penn.

Slowly and gradually Penn began to buy land from them, a piece at a time, since he felt that they were the true owners. The Indians liked to take their time making decisions, and Penn let them. Since Indian land belonged to the tribe and not to individuals, they could not sell a piece until the whole tribe consented. Gradually Penn acquired tract after tract until he had purchased the land all along the Delaware from Pennsbury down past Cape Henlopen; that included what is now the state of Delaware. Penn was not Proprietor of the Delaware portion, which he called the Three Lower Counties, but the Duke of York had granted him a limited deed to them. The deed gave Penn the right to govern them along with Pennsylvania and made him a kind of tenant with the Duke of York as his landlord.

Penn paid the Indians for the land in the kind of currency that they wanted. They could not have spent European money in the American forests. They needed blankets, woolen fabrics, kettles, coats, shirts, and stockings; hoes, knives, and hunting rifles; scissors, combs, needles, and the like, and that was what Penn gave them. The purchase price of the first piece of land (Pennsbury) included twenty gallons of rum. But as soon as Penn reached America and saw that rum was harmful to the Indians, he never again allowed it to be part of the purchase price of land.

Pennsylvania soon hummed with progress. Building went on apace. Penn had arrived in the late autumn of 1682. By the next summer there were nearly eighty houses and cottages in Philadelphia. Many of the first Quakers to come to Philadelphia were experienced merchants. They knew how to get trade started right away. They very soon had ships coming and going, and they opened up shops.

More shiploads of adventurers continued to arrive. They came faster than houses could be built for them. They camped under the trees, or they even moved into the caves in the bluffs along the river. Everyone arrived full of hope, and when they saw for themselves that all the wonderful reports about America were true, they were willing to put up with any temporary discomfort.

By the end of another year Philadelphia had 357 houses completed, some of them lovely brick mansions. She had a population of 2,500. Ships from all over the world came to her wharfs. A great yearly fair was established in the city to which the livestock and products of the province were brought. And outside of Philadelphia the big country estates and farmlands were beginning to bloom and prosper.

Nearly seventy percent of the first adventurers were English, and the rest were Welsh, Irish, Dutch, and Rhenish. Those who came from Holland and the Rhineland did so because of Penn's journeys through their countries. Germantown was settled by a group of thirteen Dutch families. Merion was settled by the Welsh. Eventually settlers came from almost everywhere.

William Penn went on doing the work of many men. He met with his Council and Assembly. He conferred with merchants. He attended Quaker meetings and worried about church affairs. He made friends with the governors of neighboring colonies: New York, New Jersey, Virginia, and Maryland.

There was only one problem with a neighboring colony that Penn could not solve. It was with Maryland. According to the wording of the royal Charters given to Lord Baltimore and to William Penn, their boundaries were confused and their lands overlapped. Further, Lord Baltimore declared that Penn didn't have any right to the Three Lower Counties.

Even before William Penn arrived in America, William Markham had had a set-to with Charles Calvert, the third Lord Baltimore, who was Proprietor of Maryland. When Markham saw how confused the situation was he decided to put it all off until William Penn reached America.

"It is a most difficult case," he explained to Penn. "Lord Baltimore's northern boundary is the fortieth degree of northern latitude according to his Charter. Yet the southern boundary of Pennsylvania, according to our Charter, is twelve miles north of New Castle, which we thought was the fortieth degree. But it lies miles south of the fortieth."

"And what progress hast thou made?" Penn asked Markham.

"None. I met with Lord Baltimore, and we came to no agreement. We cannot."

"Cannot?"

"Some of Baltimore's men came to New Castle and took a reading with a surveying instrument. They claim the fortieth degree is much farther north than anyone realized. It would even fall north of Philadelphia. We would lose our new city and our river and harbor."

William Penn sent messengers to Lord Baltimore at once, to ask Lord Baltimore to meet with him and discuss the border question. And the two proprietors did meet soon after, at West River in Maryland. The meeting was strained and unfriendly and accomplished nothing.

"A letter from the King," Penn reminded Baltimore, "gives thee two degrees measured northward from Watkin's Point. And that does not come as far north as the fortieth degree. My line is twelve miles north of New Castle, and that does not come as far north as the fortieth degree. Obviously, everyone thought the fortieth degree was farther south than it is."

Baltimore insisted on the fortieth degree and would not compromise.

Lord Baltimore raised the other quarrel that he had with Penn—the Three Lower Counties. Penn refused to let him change the subject.

"We must first settle our controversy about the line running east and west between Pennsylvania and Maryland. Then we can discuss the Three Lower Counties," he said.

The conference ended, and Penn returned to Pennsylvania.

When Penn had been in America nearly two years, his difference with Lord Baltimore was still not solved. They exchanged letters with one another, but it did no good. They both wrote to their influential friends in the government in London. It looked as though the whole unfortunate matter would have to be taken to the King's Privy Council.

"Perhaps I ought to return to England," said Penn regretfully.

He wanted to stay in America. He had a house in Philadelphia, and the house at Pennsbury was already started. He wanted Gulielma to come to America with the children. He wanted his whole family to come to America: his sister and brother-in-law Margaret and Anthony Lowther, and their children.

But when he heard that Lord Baltimore had already set sail for England, he knew he must do the same.

"I am following him as fast as I can," he wrote to the Duke of York.

With a heavy heart he prepared for the long voyage home. He appointed James Harrison to look after Pennsbury and oversee the rest of the building and landscaping. His gardener's name was Ralph Smyth. "Set out the garden by the house, plant sweet herbs, sparro grass, carrots, parsnips, artichokes, salatin, and all flowers and kitchen herbs there," he instructed his gardener. "Let a peach tree be planted between every apple tree. Let all the peaches about the grounds in Indian fields be saved, making a barrel of wine or two, and dry the rest, save that a few be preserved when almost ripe. . . . Get the walks to the house in the courts graveled. . . . Let handsome steps be made at the water side. . . ."

At last in August, 1684, he went aboard the ketch

Endeavour. It was almost as hard to say good-by to America as it had been to say good-by to England. America was fast becoming his native land. Before the ship sailed, he wrote a letter to Friends in Pennsylvania:

"My love and my life is to you, and with you; and no water can quench it, nor distance wear it out, or bring it to an end. I have been with you, cared over you and served you with unfeigned love; and you are beloved of me, and near to me, beyond utterance. . . ."

What made him happiest of all was that he had been able to unite so many kinds of people in one peaceful community. When he reached England, he would be able to report happily, "not one soldier, or arms borne, or militia man seen, since I was first in Pennsylvania."

CHAPTER TWELVE

Many Sorrows

HE ARRIVED IN ENGLAND on the sixth of October, and hurried straight home to Worminghurst. He had had letters from Guli, yes, but letters never tell all that is wanted. Letters took two and three months to cross the ocean. Often they were lost. He'd heard of Guli's illness, but he wanted her to tell him. He could not rest until he strode into the house and gathered them all into his arms—Guli, Springett, Letitia, and William, Jr. That was all. The baby born while Penn was in America had lived for only a few feeble weeks.

"It pleased the Lord to take away my little one when it was about three weeks old," said Guli. "It was a mighty great child and it was near dead when it was born, which I think it never got over."

She admitted she had been ill a long time after the birth, but she was fully recovered, she insisted. Her calmness and dignity made him love her more than ever.

"I wish thou hadst not been alone through it."

"I was not alone, beloved. Dear George Fox came apurpose to see me. Margaret Fox's son and daughter came another time, and all of our friends about Worminghurst."

In a few days Penn rode up to London. There he chatted with various members of the King's Privy Council, and at last with the King and the Duke of York. He looked at his King with a saddening heart. Charles II had been corrupted by his own power, and his health was failing too. He had dissolved Parliament for good and he was ruling by himself, determined to be an absolute monarch. He had lost interest in the colonies that lay three thousand miles away. Penn could see that it would take a long time to persuade the King and his Privy Council even to hear his case with Baltimore. It would take much longer to solve it.

"I shall be in England much longer than I expected," he told Friends. "So I shall spend my time working at my old post and province, *liberty of conscience.*"

He busied himself and used his influence to have this one or that one released from prison. There was plenty for him to do, because civil liberties were at an end. All printed matter was censored. Persecutions had grown worse, and nearly fifteen hundred Quakers were in prison all over England and Wales, not to mention other minorities.

When Penn had been in England about four months, King Charles died and his brother James II succeeded to the throne. At first, Penn had high hopes that conditions in England would improve under James. But his hopes were soon dashed. James's policies only made matters worse. The English people were in a mood to stage a serious revolt. The Whig Party became active once more.

The official Church of England was Protestant. James II was Catholic. Since the majority of the English people were Protestant, they were alarmed for fear the official church would be changed to Catholic. Anti-Catholic feeling ran high in England. Across the Channel in France the case was reversed. The official church of France was Catholic, and Protestants were being persecuted. The world was a sea of trouble.

Penn and Baltimore did manage, in spite of all the confusion, to have a few hearings before the Privy Council regarding their border disputes. Part of it was solved. The Privy Council decided to divide Delaware between the two. They drew a north-south line that gave the eastern part along the Delaware River to Penn and the western part along the Chesapeake Bay to Baltimore. But the line running east and west between Maryland and Pennsylvania was still to be worked out.

Philip Ford still handled all of Penn's financial affairs, including all his income from Pennsylvania, or as much as Penn was able to collect. Quitrents were proving hard to gather, because there was such a shortage of metal and paper money in the colonies. Penn always seemed to be in debt to Ford. No matter how much money came in, it never seemed to be enough to cover what William Penn drew from his account. Or so Ford said, and Penn believed him. The balance due Ford grew so large and lasted so long, that Ford said he wanted some kind of guaranty.

"For the sake of my family," he told Penn. "Thou must give me some security that the balance will at some time be paid."

So Penn gave him a mortgage on his personal lands in America—300,000 acres including Pennsbury.

Penn was too worried about Quaker matters to give sufficient thought to his own affairs. Ever since his return he had worried constantly about Quakers in prison. He had many conversations with King James about them. There could be no peace without freedom, he kept insisting.

At last, to his great joy, the King listened. He issued a pardon, and almost thirteen hundred Friends walked out of prison and returned to their families.

And Penn was continually worrying about Pennsylvania. He began to receive disturbing rumors and reports that the men in the Pennsylvania government were quarreling among themselves. The settlers claimed they had no way of paying their quitrents. He was needed on both sides of the ocean at once! He must go to Pennsylvania to straighten out problems there. He must remain in England until his border dispute with Maryland was settled.

The times under James II grew more confused. He was not nearly so wise and clever a man as his brother Charles II had been. He irritated first one political group and then another. At one time he issued a declaration granting all non-conformists and minorities freedom of worship. Parliament declared it wasn't legal because they hadn't approved it. The King was Catholic. The Parliament was mostly Protestant.

"Let's be patient," many Whigs said. "James has no son to inherit the throne. When he dies, the throne will go to his older daughter Mary by his first wife. She is a Protestant and married to William of Orange in Holland who is also Protestant. Even if something should happen to Mary, we are still safe, because his younger daughter Anne is also Protestant."

But King James had married for a second time. His second wife was Catholic. When the news flew around that his second wife was expecting a child the alarm was tremendous. When the child was born and proved to be a boy, a Prince of Wales, a Catholic heir to the throne, the alarm grew worse. Whig leaders, Church of England leaders, and even Royalists put their heads together. King James must be deposed!

King James went on making political blunders and

playing into the hands of the opposition. Advice of such true personal friends as William Penn did no good.

Revolt spread. Plans developed. The decision was made.

"We will invite his daughter Mary and William of Orange to come to England and be our rulers."

In November, 1688, William of Orange landed with troops on the coast of England. James was too weak a man to cope with the situation. He and his Queen and infant son fled to France. William and Mary became the new rulers of England. The Protestant Revolution had taken place without any bloodshed.

William Penn had remained loyal to James through it all. Their grandfathers had been friends; their fathers had been friends; they were friends. He had done everything he could to persuade James to follow a wise course.

After James was deposed, anyone who had been on his side was in danger of being arrested. Penn knew that. He knew that he was no longer in favor at Court, and Pennsylvania had lost her royal patron. Lord Baltimore was out of favor, too. Both Proprietors knew they would have to forget their border dispute for a good long while.

Just a few weeks after William and Mary were proclaimed rulers of England, the new Privy Council issued a warrant for William Penn's arrest "upon suspicion of high treason."

The future had never looked darker, William Penn

thought as he sat with his family at Worminghurst. If he were convicted of treason, he would probably lose his colony. If he lost his colony, what would happen to all the adventurers who had gone there seeking freedom and happiness? If he were convicted of treason—and beheaded—and his lands confiscated—what would become of his family?

He and Gulielma were deeply worried. They had four children in 1689. Their youngest was a three-year-old daughter, another Gulielma. They both looked at fourteen-year-old Springett. As the oldest son he would inherit all the lands—if the lands were not confiscated by the Crown.

William Penn was accused of conspiring with James II against King William. Penn wrote a letter to the Principal Secretary of State at once, saying, "I do profess solemnly in the presence of God, I have no hand or share in any conspiracy against the King or government, nor do I know any that have." He remained in Worminghurst, and did not go up to London to give himself up. He hoped that public hysteria would die down soon. It didn't, because James really was plotting to come back with an army and recapture his throne. So all of James's former friends were suspected of plotting along with him.

A war between England and France began that same spring, and that added to the public excitement. In the fall the child Gulielma died, and that added to the grief of the Penns.

Around the end of the year William Penn moved his

family to Hammersmith, near London. Today Hammersmith is part of the city of London, but then it was a nearby village. They stayed there during the winter while Penn appealed to everyone in the government that he considered his friend.

"I must appear before the Privy Council for questioning," he told Gulielma.

"We must rely on God's mercy."

After hours of tedious and tiring questions, questions, questions, he was at last cleared of the charge and set free.

He rushed home and announced, "Now we can go to America!"

There was no further reason for remaining in England. He could do nothing at Court; he could do nothing about his border dispute with Baltimore. His wife's health had been badly affected by the trials they were going through.

"The brisk climate of the New World will restore thee," he declared.

It was not to be. Not yet. The following June he was charged with treason again, actually arrested, and placed in the Tower of London for two weeks.

Philip Ford saw a golden opportunity to take advantage of Penn, and Bridget Ford egged her husband on. Ford came to Penn as soon as he was out of the Tower.

"Thou may still be tried for treason," he reminded Penn dolefully. "What of those who depend upon thee?"

Penn didn't need to be reminded of that. "I must trust in God," he told Ford. "He knows I am innocent."

"Thou hast many enemies. Men in public life always do."

Penn nodded.

Why not, Ford suggested, transfer the whole Province of Pennsylvania into Philip Ford's name? Secretly, of course.

"What about my family?" Penn argued.

"What about every family in Pennsylvania?" Ford retorted. "None will know but thee, me, and Bridget. I will not even mention it in my last will and testament."

They discussed the idea for a long while, and at last Penn consented. He was still heavily in debt to Ford, or thought he was. Ford drew up a paper that Penn understood to be a mortgage, and he signed it. He hoped, in that way, to protect the colonists, in case his lands were confiscated by the Crown. And they would be if he was convicted of treason.

Once more Penn was cleared of the treason charge, and once more he began to make plans for going to America. He even started to gather a group of adventurers. But Whitehall could not leave Penn alone. They could not forget what a close personal friend he had been of James and the whole Stuart family. Queen Mary issued a proclamation ordering his arrest.

Again the disappointment and worry! Gulielma was wilting under the pressures. Penn could see her health growing frailer from day to day. How could he ever clear his name? How could he do anything else until he *had* cleared his name? False witnesses had even come forward to testify to his guilt.

"I cannot administer Pennsylvania or look after my family from inside the Tower of London," Penn decided. "And I certainly cannot do anything for anybody without my head."

He then and there decided to go into hiding until he could find a way to clear his name. No one knows, even to this day, where he was living for the next three years; none but his family and most trusted friends.

The Penn family was descending into utter poverty. The Irish lands had dwindled away from neglect. What money they had, had been going into the Pennsylvania project for years, since Penn had gone into it entirely at his own expense. He had thought the quitrents would support him, but they never did.

Sorrows continued to pile up. William and Mary took over the government of Pennsylvania and appointed a military man, Benjamin Fletcher, as Captain General of Pennsylvania. So his colony, the great experiment in peaceful living, was to have military rule! And Guli's health was failing. For that matter Springett was far from robust.

Springett was a great source of comfort in these times of trouble. He was old enough to understand, a serious, sensitive, deeply religious lad.

During the three years that Penn was in hiding, he occupied his time with writing. He wrote many episcles and two important tracts. One was *An Essay Towards the Present and Future Peace of Europe.* In it he recommended an international parliament to keep peace between nations. War was wasteful, he wrote. It caused poverty and sickness and destroyed property. If the kings and princes of Europe could only realize it, they would be much more prosperous and happy if they united to make peace. His second tract was called *Some Fruits of Solitude,* or it is sometimes called *Reflections and Maxims.* It is a collection of wise sayings and advice.

Cautiously and slowly Penn began to consult this friend and that about ways and means of clearing his name. After sufficient time had passed an influential friend, Henry Sydney, did lay Penn's case before the King. He noted that the King's attitude was beginning to soften. William Penn's brother-in-law brought Sydney to Penn's hiding place.

"Please tell King William that I am a true and faithful servant to King William and Queen Mary," Penn told Sydney. "I know of no plot."

Many more months passed. One important person after another spoke to the King in Penn's behalf, and at last their persistent appeals took effect. Three Lords, the Lords Rochester, Ranelagh, and Sydney, appeared before King William and asked the King to consider Penn's case. It was based on false testimony, they explained. The King nodded his head and agreed. He told his Secretary of State to advise Penn that he was a free man.

The hiding was over! The arrest warrants were

ended! He could move about freely and sit among his friends in Meeting for Worship.

One more sorrow awaited him. Gulielma had been ill for months, and even the good news of his freedom could not restore her. He spent most of his time at her bedside, watching her grow weaker. January passed and February advanced. Guli's relatives and children gathered round her. On the twenty-third of February, 1694, she began to sink rapidly and was soon gone.

"She was an excelling person, both as child, wife, mother, mistress, friend and neighbor," said William Penn.

After Guli had been laid to rest, he took his three children back to the big, rambling manor house at Worminghurst.

CHAPTER THIRTEEN

Hannah Callowhill

NOT FOR MANY WEEKS did William Penn feel like seeing anyone or going up to London. His energies were spent from years of worry and grief. But by summer time he began to move about and be his old self. Nineteen-year-old Springett was at his side most of the time and shared all of his thoughts. Father and son talked often of Pennsylvania.

"Now that my name is cleared," William Penn said to his son, "I am going to petition the Crown. I shall request the return of my colony's government."

When Queen Mary read Penn's petition asking her to restore his colony to him, she nodded and turned it over to her advisers. Penn soon had his answer.

"The Pennsylvania colony shall be restored to William Penn on two conditions," said Whitehall. "First, he must promise to contribute to the defense of the colonies; and second, he must go to America to govern the colony in person."

The war with France was still going on, and in America the French and English were bitter rivals. The idea of raising a militia in Pennsylvania was a hard one for a Quaker to accept. Even though Whitehall wanted only eighty militiamen from Pennsylvania or their equivalent cost in cash, the Quaker majority in the Pennsylvania Assembly would be reluctant. On the other hand, if Penn did not consent to a small militia, Pennsylvania would continue to be ruled by a military governor. With a heavy heart, Penn consented.

To the second promise—to go to America in person—he consented with a light and happy heart.

In a royal grant, dated August 20, 1694, issued by King William and Queen Mary, the administration of the province and its territories was restored to William Penn.

He began to show his old vigor and enthusiasm once more as he bustled about and talked of transporting his whole household across the Atlantic. He was short of funds, and the move would be costly. He wrote to

William Markham, who was once more Deputy Governor, and urged him to try to collect quitrents.

Soon after his colony was restored to him, William Penn set out on a traveling minister's journey through western England, visiting Friends' meetings. Wherever he spoke he drew large crowds.

"Since it hath pleased God and the King to give me my liberty, I have been willing to visit my friends before my going for America, and in those places especially where I have suffered most in my character, by common fame, stirred up by ignorance or prejudice, that if it were possible I might do my profession, person and posterity that right of appearing another and better man than I have too often been represented."

The city of Bristol was a big center of Quakerism and Penn knew most of the Quaker families there. He had gone through Bristol on his trips to Ireland, and he had gone to Bristol to see off the first shipload of Pennsylvania adventurers. But he had never lingered quite so long in Bristol before. Everyone knew why. He was spending a great deal of time—before and after meetings, at dinners, in the evenings—visiting with the Callowhill family. The Callowhills were modest folk. Thomas Callowhill was a linen draper, and he and his wife and daughter, Hannah, lived on High Street in a house that was adequate and comfortable, but nothing compared to the scale of place that Penn was used to.

William Penn, lonely widower with three children at home (the youngest of which was still only fourteen), had discovered Hannah Callowhill—with some contriving from the members of the meeting. Hannah was twenty years younger than he, shy, and startled that so important a man should pay attention to her.

"Oh, no!" she gasped to her friends when they encouraged her. "He is much too grand. The idea is impossible!"

"It is not impossible, Hannah," they urged. "We can tell that he loves thee, and thou wouldst make him a splendid wife."

When Penn finally arrived back in Worminghurst, his whole household was watching for him. Penn began at once a happy account of all his experiences in the towns and cities where he had spoken. But most of his report was about Hannah Callowhill. Springett and Tishe looked at each other and winked. So *that* was how it was!

Letters began to travel the post roads between Bristol and Worminghurst, all through the summer months. Penn sent Hannah's mother a recipe for drying fruit. He sent her father some legal advice. He sent letter after letter to Hannah, declaring his love in every way he could think of.

Come autumn, and William Penn announced that he felt called to go on another speaking mission—in the general direction of Bristol.

"And you three are to go with me."

Merrily Springett, Tishe, and Bille began to pack and prepare for the trip. A visit among the Friends' meetings of western England would be good for them, their father declared. And they agreed.

There was always a stir and a hubbub around Penn, and when four Penns arrived in Bristol there was considerably more. Springett was the only quiet one. Tishe and Bille were full of energy like their father. At Bristol they lodged at the home of Richard Snead, and Penn went calling immediately upon the Callowhills.

He swept the shy Hannah off her feet. The consent that he could not win from her by mail, he won in a few days in person. On the eleventh of November they appeared before the Monthly Meeting to declare their intention to wed.

Since they would have to appear before Monthly Meeting a second time, Penn remained in Bristol another month and whiled away the days by speaking at meetings in nearby towns. At Wells, a town seventeen miles south of Bristol, he drew a particularly large crowd. He had planned to speak in the main hall of the inn, but his audience overflowed into the street. In order to be heard both indoors and out, Penn preached from a balcony. It was not hard for petty officials, still hostile to the Quakers, to interpret such an incident as an unlawful and riotous assembly. The Mayor quickly issued an arrest warrant for Penn, and officers reached the scene while the meeting was still in progress. Charge? The place was not properly licensed. Rudely they seized Penn, rudely refused to let him finish his sermon, roughly they dragged him before the magistrates. But they were defeated with gentleness when Penn produced his proper certificate for the meeting.

"I can see," sighed Hannah Callowhill, "that life with William Penn will never be dull."

As soon as plans for the wedding were made, the four Penns went home to Worminghurst. They were to return to Bristol in January for the ceremony. But that winter illness struck the Penn household and upset everyone's plans. One after another they came down with the grippe. And not just the Penns. An epidemic went through the whole community. Damp, cold, snowy weather helped it along. Letitia did not catch it, but Penn and his two sons were laid up for weeks.

Penn's chief worry was his bride-to-be. After all, he was fifty-one, and she was twenty years younger. Would she understand why he had not been able to appear for his own wedding? He wrote her letter after letter.

"I intend as fast as I can, to make thee my most dear wife, and to love, prize and tender thee above all my worldly comforts."

Of course, Hannah understood. She wrote to tell him how worried she was about him and his children.

Gradually William Penn and Bille recovered, but Springett did not. His cough held on, and he was still not well when the entire family set out for Bristol the end of February.

At another large and happy gathering William Penn was married once more, this time to Hannah Callowhill.

The wedding took place on the fifth of March, 1696.

Hannah Callowhill proved a blessing to the household at once. It had been rather badly managed for two years, but as soon as Hannah arrived things began to run smoothly again. She was a loving and sympathetic nurse as well, and she put the ailing and coughing Springett back into bed.

"Thou must rest and recover," she told him.

Springett was sicker than anyone realized. In spite of the care that his stepmother gave him, his strength failed. Soon he and everyone else realized that he could not recover.

Just twenty-one! Pennsylvania's future Proprietor!

"I am resigned," he told the family gathered around him.

On the tenth of April he breathed his last.

It was a crushing blow to Penn to lose that eldest, most promising son. His heir was now William Penn, Jr., sixteen, who was proving himself a troublesome, irresponsible, and unruly lad.

But griefs heal, and the living go on.

William Penn had to find a way to take his family to America. Whitehall would not let him keep his colony otherwise. Once in America they could live at Pennsbury which was large enough to support them. Penn was more in debt to Ford than ever; the balance was now more than ten thousand pounds.

Penn decided to go over to Ireland and look at his estates. Perhaps something could be salvaged. But he returned from Ireland to report that his lands there were almost ruined. He would have to sell a few pieces of land in America to raise the money he needed, and he could sell some of the timber off the Worminghurst land.

But nearly four years had passed from the time of his wedding to Hannah before Penn was able to arrange the trip to America. During that time William, Jr., married Mary Jones of Bristol. The couple were to live at Worminghurst after the rest of the family departed for America. And during those same years the war with France ended, making the high seas safe for travel once more. It seemed as though everything was at last solved. After years of strife, the founder of Pennsylvania could look forward to peace and freedom and happiness.

There was still one dark shadow in the picture: the Fords. Penn spent an afternoon with Philip and Bridget Ford to say farewell to them and give them some last-minute instructions. The afternoon was pleasant enough, but just before Penn arose to leave, the Fords went off by themselves and whispered together. Then they came back to Penn.

" 'Twould be better if thou gave us some money before departing," they said.

Philip Ford added, "And there is a paper that I signed regarding errors in the accounts. I should like it back."

Penn stared at them in surprise. Perhaps he could furnish them with additional funds, but the paper! It was amongst his things at Worminghurst, and he didn't have time to search it out. He knew perfectly well what it was. Long ago Ford had signed an agreement to make good any errors in the accounts. That is, if he made any mistakes in his figures that short-changed Penn, Ford agreed to pay the amount.

"I cannot lay my hands on that paper now," Penn said.

"Then thou must give me another paper to cancel that one," declared Ford, and he whipped out a paper all prepared for Penn's signature.

Penn refused. That was the only protection his wife and family had if anything happened to him.

Ford grew angry and threatening. What of the Ford family if anything should happen to Penn?

"If thou dost not sign I shall expose thee," said Ford. "I shall tell all the world about our secret arrangement of having the title of Pennsylvania in my name instead of yours."

Penn gasped.

Once again Ford had waited until just before sailing time. He knew Penn didn't have time to think of a solution. He knew Penn couldn't postpone his trip any longer. He had delayed too many years already. The Crown had given him back his colony on the promise that he go to America in person to govern it. The Crown wasn't going to wait forever.

William Penn paced up and down in silence for a moment. Then, wheeling around, he seized the paper and signed it, hoping that some divine providence would save him.

In another few days he and Hannah and Letitia were aboard the *Canterbury* at Cowes in southern England. On September 3, 1699, the ship weighed anchor and set sail for America.

CHAPTER FOURTEEN

Penn's Second Trip to America

THE PENNS WERE TOSSED ABOUT at sea for three months, and the longer the wind and weather held them up the more excited and impatient William Penn became to see America again. True, he had exchanged a multitude of letters with the colonists, especially the men in the government. But he wanted to see for himself how much had been accomplished in fifteen years.

With him aboard the *Canterbury* was a young man

of twenty-five named James Logan, from County Armagh, Ireland. Logan's parents had been Scottish Quakers, and he had been starting out as a merchant when Penn asked him to be his personal secretary. Logan was a very learned and brilliant young man, and Penn had been deeply impressed by him. Over the years, James Logan became Penn's most devoted and trusted friend, as well as Secretary of the Province of Pennsylvania.

When the *Canterbury* finally eased her way into Delaware Bay and up the river past New Castle to Chester, the shores were crowded with colonists and Indians. Many had traveled great distances to welcome their Proprietor home. The Penns stepped ashore at Chester to a hubbub of cheers, speeches, handshakes, and happy commotion. They went on to Philadelphia in carriages and they stayed temporarily at the home of Edward Shippen.

As William Penn drove through the streets of Philadelphia, his pulse raced and his heart pounded. He beheld wide, lovely streets, and seven hundred houses, most of them brick and surrounded by gardens and trees. Along the river front there were ample quays for ships of trade to come and go—carrying away linen, hemp, potash, whale oil, lumber, furs, tobacco, and even copper and iron—bringing back all the manufactured things that were displayed in the shops. And he beheld market places, churches, schools. Philadelphia was already the second largest city in the New World. Only Boston was larger.

He took hold of Hannah's hand. "My sufferings have all been worth-while," he said. "Just see what God hath wrought of them."

The Penn family soon moved into the Slate Roof House on Second Street. It had been built by the wealthy Quaker merchant, Samuel Carpenter, and was divided into several apartments. James Logan was able to have an apartment in the same building. In the Slate Roof House, on January 28, 1700, Hannah's first child, John Penn, was born. He was the only one of Penn's children born in the New World, and he soon became known as John the American.

With James Logan at his side, Penn plunged into the governmental affairs of the colony at once. He met with the Assembly. He met with his Council. With them he considered revisions in the laws. He traveled around the colony and down into Delaware. He was as thrilled as he had been by his first glimpse of Philadelphia. There were still no militia patrolling the borders and no bristling stockades guarding the towns. The Indians in the surrounding areas were still friendly. In fact, when Indian tribes had differences among themselves, they came to Penn for advice. Around the countryside more and more prosperous acres were being cultivated.

By June his country home, Pennsbury Manor, was ready, and he took Hannah, Letitia, and John up the Delaware in a barge to their new home.

Today anyone may visit Pennsbury Manor and see the kind of home that he built. It has been carefully and accurately restored by the Pennsylvania Historical and Museum Commission, who went back to the original letters and instructions written by Penn. The house is of red brick, three stories high, with a tile shingled roof. Its casement windows look out at the Delaware River. And from the front door to the water's edge there is a long walk lined with poplar trees. About the house there are flower gardens, herb gardens, fruit trees, a dipping well, and bake and brew house. Indoors, the rooms are the same as in his day, with wainscoted walls and pale green tiles framing the fireplaces.

Pennsbury Manor became a center of hospitality. Governors of other colonies came there to visit. The Indian tribes came there for conferences. Penn traveled down to Philadelphia frequently in his barge.

"At last our lives are settled and we are done with troubles and poverty," the Penns thought.

Happily they read letters from William Penn, Jr., telling them of their first grandchild, another Gulielma, born shortly after they left England. And then, in their second winter in America, they received news of a second grandchild, named Springett.

But their happy life in America lasted only two years. Political rumblings in far off London warned Penn that there was a movement afoot to make Pennsylvania a royal colony. Virginia, New Hampshire, New York, and Massachusetts were already royal colonies. Lord Baltimore had lost his proprietorship and was living in Maryland as a private citizen. War was brewing again between France and England. That would mean war between the French and English colonies in America. If Pennsylvania refused to wage war on her neighbors, and she probably would refuse, that would be a perfect excuse for taking the colony away from Penn and appointing a military governor once more.

Penn realized that he must return to London.

"It will be but a short stay," he said to Hannah. "I shall return to thee as fast as ever I can."

Hannah shook her head. "Thy last return to England was for but a short while, and it grew to fifteen years."

Hannah had never really liked country life. She was used to busy Bristol. Worminghurst had been lonely and remote, and so was Pennsbury. She longed to return to the bustle of a city. To be left behind at Pennsbury with nothing but the forests for company? No indeed! So the whole family planned to return to England.

Hannah was well liked in America, and the colonists were sorry to see her go.

Important men always have enemies who are jealous of them and would like to destroy or defeat them. William Penn had his share of enemies on both sides of the ocean. But once in London, he would be able to talk to members of the Privy Council personally and give them a truer idea of the situation in America.

"And I can make them realize," he said, "how much prosperous trade Pennsylvania has created for the mother country. I can remind them that I have developed Pennsylvania at my own expense. No other Proprietor has done that. My entire fortune has been lost into it. Instead of enriching me it pays not the debt the Crown owed my father, but involved me in twenty thousand pounds to bring it to pass."

Penn appointed Andrew Hamilton to be Lieutenant Governor of Pennsylvania. Hamilton was a proprietor of East New Jersey and had been Governor of both the Jerseys. James Logan became Secretary of the Province of Pennsylvania and Clerk of the Council.

William and Hannah Penn, Letitia, and the infant John were aboard the *Dolmahoy* on November 3, 1701.

CHAPTER FIFTEEN

Philip Ford's Betrayal

BACK TO NOISY, CROWDED LONDON, and to all the confusions of politics in high places. William Penn was in his middle fifties. He wasn't as energetic as he had once been. He had reached the age when he longed more and more for the peace and quiet of the country. But there were other things to be considered than himself. Thousands of settlers in Pennsylvania depended upon him.

Hannah Penn was expecting another child, and so

she took little John and went to stay at her parents' home in Bristol. William Penn found a place to live in Kensington, close to London, and Tishe kept house for him. He visited the Callowhills at Bristol as often as he could.

Penn hurried down to Worminghurst to see his grandchildren very soon after his arrival in England.

"A sweet girl and a Saracen of a boy!" he declared.

He had another reason for hurrying to Worminghurst. He hoped that his son and heir, William Penn, Jr., would be a more serious fellow, now that he was a married man with two children.

But William Penn the Younger was still an irresponsible fellow who liked to boast and talk. Penn the Elder wanted to share Pennsylvania's troubles with him, since he would be Proprietor some day. But the father had to face the fact that his son was not man enough for the job. Sorrowfully the aging Proprietor returned to London to shoulder the whole task himself.

Penn knew he had very little influence at Whitehall. Queen Mary had died, and King William was ruling by himself. King William was busy planning his war with France. He was not going to be very friendly toward a colony that did not want to do its share in the war.

Penn's troubles began to pile up again. Philip Ford had died in January, 1702, right after Penn's return to England. In a few months, Bridget Ford began to annoy William Penn.

"Thou owest my late husband a great sum of money," she said.

"James Logan is doing his best to gather in quitrents for me," Penn explained to her. "He is even planning to accept grains and furs and other products from the colonists instead of money. He will ship these things to me here, and I can sell them. Then there will be money."

Bridget was impatient and unpleasant. Soon she was back with another item.

"According to my husband's will," she announced, "his Pennsylvania interests will have to be sold to settle the estate."

His Pennsylvania interests? But Ford had promised Penn that he would not say anything in his last will and testament about Pennsylvania!

William Penn realized then—at long last—that the Fords had betrayed his confidence completely. He consulted two learned Quakers about it, and they sat down with Penn and went through all of his papers and accounts. They soon came up with the shocking discovery that Philip Ford had been stealing money from Penn for years and years. He had done it with cunning—and illegal—bookkeeping. He had charged eight percent interest, when the legal rate was six. He had charged Penn interest on the money he had advanced to Penn, but he had not charged himself interest on the money he was minding for Penn. He had charged interest upon interest. He had charged Penn huge commissions for being his agent. When the Quakers examined the document that Penn had signed when he was under a treason charge, they shook their heads sadly.

"This document is no mortgage," they said to Penn. "We fear it may give the Fords title to Pennsylvania. We fear it is a deed."

The Fords—Bridget Ford and her children, Philip, Jr., and two daughters—grew cocky.

"If Mr. Penn wishes his colony back," they declared, "he must pay us the whole balance that he owes us."

By then, fourteen thousand pounds!

Penn's friends sat down and figured up the accounts all over again, leaving out Ford's tricky bookkeeping. When they got through they found that Penn owed Ford only about four thousand pounds.

"I am willing to pay the four thousand," said William Penn, "to clear up this matter."

The Fords refused to listen. They wanted the whole fourteen thousand, not a shilling less.

In the spring of 1702 King William died, and Anne became Queen of England. Queen Anne was a Stuart. James II, William Penn's close friend, had been her father. William Penn was once more a favorite at court. He could stop worrying about having his colony made into a Crown colony.

Queen Anne believed in toleration and freedom of ideas. That meant religious freedom for everyone. Life in England became much happier and freer during her reign. William Penn came and went at Court.

That same spring his son, Thomas Penn, was born at Thomas Callowhill's house in Bristol.

Penn was sinking deeper and deeper into poverty. His son William was no help; he liked a gay life and fine clothes. James Logan had shipped flour, pork, fur pelts, and other items to Penn on two ships. But the war between England and France had started soon after Anne became Queen. The high seas were full of danger. One ship was captured by the enemy and the cargo of the other ship was stolen by the crew. There didn't seem to be any way of collecting the money due Penn from America.

That summer Letitia was married to William Aubrey at Worminghurst, and her wedding brought the whole Penn family together for a while and filled the house with guests and good cheer. Hannah did not return to Bristol for several weeks.

"I am tired of living so much apart from thee," Hannah told her husband.

He promised her that they would have a home near London as soon as he could arrange it. Meanwhile he found himself lodgings in London.

The next spring their third grandchild, William Penn III, was born at Worminghurst, and their daughter Hannah was born in the summer at Bristol.

Hannah began to lose patience. She was tired of living with her parents and visiting with her own husband. She wrote Penn a serious letter about it, reminding him that now he had three children who scarcely knew him. John was nearly four, Thomas was a year-

and-a-half, and the new baby, Hannah, was nearly three months old, and he had not seen her at all.

Penn wrote back to say that his poverty was to blame. "As soon as my business with the Fords is cleared up we can all return to America and live at Pennsbury in comfort," he promised, and he went out to Bristol for a long visit with her and the children. In November, 1704, they had another child, Margaret.

Meanwhile he had sent William, Jr., to America hoping that the change of scene would get him away from his gay companions in England. Perhaps when the young man saw the great province he was going to inherit, he would feel inspired to settle down. But young Penn only fell into other bad company in Philadelphia, and none of the Proprietor's trusted friends there could do anything with him. He was even arrested for making a commotion in a tavern. James Logan wrote often to Penn the Elder about him. At last the lad returned to England, and his heartbroken father wrote,

"O Pennsylvania! what hast thou cost me? Above thirty thousand pounds more than ever I got by it, two hazardous and most fatiguing voyages, my straits and slavery here, and my child's soul almost . . ."

William Penn fell ill and needed many weeks to recover.

He was deeply worried about Pennsylvania. He began to talk to this member and that of the Privy Council about turning the colony over to the Crown. Under Queen Anne it would be safe. The Crown could pay him a sum of money for the government and that would clear up his debts, settle with the Fords, and leave money enough to take care of his family.

The Fords had been harassing him constantly for three years. The Quakers were doing their best to bring about a settlement. But at last Penn and his Quaker advisers agreed that it would have to go to a court of law. As the lawyers worked on it, they began to worry for fear Penn could not win. Penn was confident that he could.

"When the court examines those dishonest accounts, they will decide in my favor," he declared.

"But thou has signed approvals of the accounts so often, Friend William!"

Realizing that the case would keep Penn in London a long time, Hannah gathered up her children and came to London. She returned to Bristol only briefly in January, 1706, when their fifth child, Richard, was born. She came back soon afterward, and the whole family settled in a house in Ealing, a suburb of London. Their next child, Dennis, was born there a year later.

The Ford case dragged on in Chancery Court for three years. Penn's lawyers were worried. Their worst fears soon came true. At the end of 1707, Chancery Court decided against Penn. They said that, because the accounts went back so far, and because Penn had signed so many papers approving them without examining them, the old accounts could not be opened. They must stand.

What was Penn to do? He was no longer a young

man. He had a second family of small children depending upon him. His friends knew he had been done a terrible injustice by the Fords, but they could do nothing if the court decided otherwise.

How cocky and boastful the Fords were after that triumph in court! And they still had that deed. They decided to push Penn still further, claiming that he owed them rent on the Province. After all, didn't they *own* Pennsylvania? Wasn't Penn just a tenant there? And they won another decision, in the Court of Common Pleas, that Penn did owe them three years' rent. Nearly three thousand pounds!

"I shall not pay it," Penn announced. "I plan to appeal the whole matter to the House of Lords."

The meeting for worship was always a source of comfort and strength. The Penns were there every First Day, unless ill health or traveling difficulties kept them away.

On January 7, 1708, William Penn sat in the silent meeting at Gracechurch Street in London—the old meeting house where he had once been arrested as a young man. While the meeting was deep in its silent worship, bailiffs appeared, under orders from the Fords to arrest Penn. Penn's friends were horrified at such an undignified thing. Could not the Fords at least wait until meeting for worship was over? They hurried the bailiffs outside and promised that Penn would come voluntarily. There was no need to drag him away.

William Penn was sixty-three; his health was failing; but he was determined not to pay the unjust charge to the Fords. So, later that day, he reported to the Fleet, London's famous debtors' prison. Once more he became a prisoner for the sake of his conscience.

He did not have to stay in the crowded, filthy prison itself. He was allowed to have lodgings nearby. Hannah gathered up her children once more and took them out to Bristol to her family. Then she hurried back to London and found a place to live as close to the prison as possible.

The Fords were so proud of themselves they were utterly unbearable. But they had gone too far in imprisoning a man like Penn who was so well known and loved, although they didn't realize it. They went even further. They declared they had the right to govern Pennsylvania, and they petitioned Queen Anne for a new royal Charter that would turn the Proprietorship over to them. That was more than anyone could bear. The Queen's advisers declared that the government of Pennsylvania had never been part of the case. They advised the Queen not to answer, and the Fords received a severe rebuff. At that the Fords became really frightened.

Meanwhile, leading Quakers, including Thomas Callowhill, had put their heads together. They invited the Fords to arbitrate, and the Fords were frightened enough to listen. Nine Quakers offered the Fords sixty-seven hundred pounds as a final settlement. The Fords accepted. Penn gave the nine Quakers a new mortgage, this time a genuine mortgage, on the Province.

The skies were clear at last, for the first time in

many, many years! Penn was out of debtors' prison. The Fords were gone. He had his colony and could arrange to sell it to the Crown. Pennsbury still waited for him, and for his wife and children.

"I hope next spring, if not next fall, to set forth."

CHAPTER SIXTEEN

The Closing Years

"FIRST WE MUST FIND a house to live in," said the practical Hannah.

The Penns moved to Ruscombe, about halfway between London and Oxford, and very near the city of Reading. They took a big house in the wooded countryside, the kind of place Penn liked. There a large family gathered. There were William and Hannah Penn and five children. The baby Hannah had died. With them were the wife and three children of William

Penn, Jr. The irresponsible younger Penn had gone airily off to Europe.

From Ruscombe, Proprietor Penn corresponded with James Logan and other government men in Pennsylvania. He made an occasional trip to London to keep in touch with matters there. He was arranging the sale of his government to the Crown. On First Day mornings, he and his family drove in to Reading to the meeting for worship.

When he had been at Ruscombe about a year, Penn was taken ill on one of his visits to London. We think today it was a mild stroke. He recovered from it, but the incident alarmed him. What about Pennsylvania? He then did something very hard for a father to do. He drew up a new will, taking the Proprietorship of Pennsylvania away from his irresponsible son, William, Jr. The young man would still inherit the properties due him, but the government of Pennsylvania would be handled by two responsible trustees, and Hannah Penn would be executor of the will.

Meanwhile the Crown had agreed upon the terms for accepting the government of Pennsylvania. The purchase price was twelve thousand pounds, and Penn received a thousand of it immediately. But the final agreement was never signed.

In October, 1712, while William and Hannah Penn were visiting at Bristol, Penn suffered another stroke. He was writing a letter to James Logan, when the quill dropped from his hand, and he fell forward on his desk.

In January Hannah was able to take him to London,

but when they returned to Ruscombe he was exhausted. Another stroke soon followed that made him incompetent. He lost his memory and could speak only a few disconnected words. From then on he had to be cared for like a child. His strength slowly faded, and on July 30, 1718, between two and three in the morning, he died.

When William Penn became an invalid, Hannah Penn took charge of his affairs, and she proved herself a very capable business woman. During the years following Penn's death, the Pennsylvania colony prospered, an ever-growing monument to its creator. William Penn will always be remembered as a leader and planner of great vision who proved that free and honorable men can live together in peace.

Notes

A biography contains the message of a human life. It seeks out some former great person and makes him live again in our own times. It gives us the opportunity to find real inspiration and encouragement in the faith and deeds of a great man or woman.

When I began to examine the life of William Penn, I had no idea how much inspiring material I was going to find. Here, I soon discovered, was one of the greatest men in the history of colonial America, and he was practically unknown to us as a person. Wherever I looked I uncovered new facts, and the more I uncovered the greater he became.

I began my search for William Penn by reading the history of England, since that was his native land, and since Pennsylvania was an English colony. Then I went on a journey through England and the other countries in which he spent his time: Ireland, Holland, Germany, and France; and finally back to America to complete the task. Everything that I read and every place that I visited deepened my understanding—and my admiration.

There was the Tower of London, gruesome old prison, still guarded by men in scarlet uniforms and white neck ruffs; and not far from the Tower the church of All Hallows Barking where Penn was baptized as an infant. The church when I was there was covered with scaffolding, because it had been bombed during World War II and was just then being restored. I took a London bus out to Chigwell in Essex one pleasant afternoon, and found the original school building, made of uneven hand-made red bricks. The headmaster took me into the classroom where Penn learned his first Latin and Greek. Even though the windows have been enlarged to let in more light, it is still a dingy, oppressive place with its heavy oak-beamed ceiling. School was a grim and serious matter when Penn was a lad.

My visit to Christ Church in Oxford was a very different experience from Chigwell. Christ Church is a lovely sight. Mr. Pitz, the artist who made the illustrations for this book, has drawn a corner of the quadrangle at the head of Chapter Three. The three-storied portion in the picture is the dining hall where the hundred young men ate so boisterously at long wooden tables. The spire rising in back of the wall is the Anglican Cathedral where the services were held that Penn and his nonconformist Friends refused to attend.

A train ride brought me to Sussex in southern England and the site of Penn's Worminghurst house, where he lived for so many years. There is still a shell of the house standing, and I could see that it had been a great, roomy place, again of red brick, since timber was scarce in England. But it was the location of the house that told me so much about William Penn—high on a hill with vast panorama of the countryside. Yes, this was the kind of place Penn would have chosen. He was a man of tremendous imagination, who took a wide, liberal view of things.

And Ireland! A romantic land, lush and green and hilly, with a mild climate. There the Penn family lived in exile rather than renounce their beliefs. Macroom Castle, a big, square, gray-stoned structure, looks rather desolate and deserted with its windows boarded up. The countryside around the castle, even three centuries later, is still rather scantily populated. As I walked about the castle grounds, I could tell how lonely the Penns must have been, how they must have missed the hustle of London life, and how they must have welcomed Thomas Loe's visit.

In America, just as in Europe, modern progress has changed the landscape that Penn knew, but Pennsylvania has retained some of her forested and mountainous landscape. To me the one place in Pennsylvania that best expresses Penn's personality is Pennsbury Manor. He created it during the same years that he was creating the government of Pennsylvania. The government expressed his statesmanship. Pennsbury expresses his personal side. The manor is withdrawn, twenty-five miles up the river from Philadelphia, because he liked peaceful seclusion. The house is big with ample rooms; it is surrounded by acres of land and has a sweeping view of the surrounding country. The herb and vegetable gardens, the orchards, the bake and brew house, the well-equipped kitchen, show that Penn liked to live well and to entertain generously.

In all of these places that I visited, William Penn loomed tall and impressive, a powerful personality, a man dedicated to the rest of mankind, a man who could see farther ahead than others. As I traveled about or sat and read letters written in his own big, scrawling handwriting—in London and in Philadelphia—I knew I had found a subject who played a tremendous and exciting role in human destiny. What is more exciting, he plays that role today. His ideas are still up-to-date.

I feel that William Penn is one of the finest heroes I have ever been privileged to present to young people.

Catherine Owens Peare

Brooklyn, New York, February, 1958

Index

About the Author

Catherine Owens Peare has been writing books for young people for many years—*William Penn* is her fifteenth book—and she has been interested in writing as far back as she can remember.

She was born in Perth Amboy, New Jersey, and when she was very young her family moved to the northern part of the state, to the town of Norwood. She went to Tenafly High School and completed her education at the New Jersey State Teachers College at Montclair. But when she graduated from college, teaching posts were very scarce, and so she found a position with an investment house in Wall Street. Investments became her area of work during the day, and she wrote in her spare time.

Eventually her teacher training and her writing combined into books for young people. Her first major writing project for them was interracial—a biography of the most outstanding individual of different races. First came Albert Einstein, then Mahatma Gandhi, then Mary McLeod Bethune. By the time she had finished the life of Mrs. Bethune she was able to leave her position and free lance. Now she lives in Brooklyn and devotes all of her time to writing.